W9-ACL-429

Resource Communities:
A Decade of Disruption

WITHDRAWN

North Dakota State University Libraries

GIFT FROM

Department of Agribusiness and
Applied Economics
2009

Also of Interest

Paradoxes of Western Energy Development: How Can We Maintain the Land and the People If We Develop? edited by Cyrus M. McKell et al.

Guide to Social Impact Assessment, Kristi Branch, Douglas A. Hooper, James Thompson, and James Creighton

Social Impact Assessment and Monitoring: A Guide to the Literature, Michael J. Carley and Eduardo Bustelo

Women and the Social Costs of Economic Development: Two Colorado Case Studies, Elizabeth Moen, Elise Boulding, Jane Lillydahl, and Risa Palm

The Socioeconomic Impact of Resource Development: Methods for Assessment, F. Larry Leistritz and Steven Murdock

†*What Happened to Fairbanks? The Effects of the Trans-Alaska Oil Pipeline on the Community of Fairbanks, Alaska*, Mim Dixon

†Available in hardcover and paperback.

About the Book and Editors

Resource Communities: A Decade of Disruption
edited by Don D. Detomasi and John W. Gartrell

This volume consists of eleven original papers that survey the state of the art in research and public policy regarding specific problems and opportunities confronted by resource communities. The papers are international in scope, dealing with the experiences of resource communities in four nations—Canada, Norway, the United Kingdom, and the United States.

The decade 1972 - 1982 was a turbulent one for resource development in the Western industrialized nations. The environmental movement led to state and national systems of regulation and control over this type of activity during the early years of the decade, and rapid economic growth and the energy crisis stimulated resource development, particularly energy resource development, on an unprecedented scale during the middle years. Finally, the end of the decade witnessed a dramatic decline in resource development as a result of severe economic recession and an energy surplus. The effects of these sudden and significant changes have been felt most sharply by resource communities—the small, often isolated and dependent towns that are the focus of this book.

Don D. Detomasi is dean and professor of economics in environmental design at the University of Calgary. **John W. Gartrell** is a professor of sociology at the University of Alberta.

Resource Communities: A Decade of Disruption

edited by Don D. Detomasi and John W. Gartrell

Westview Press / Boulder and London

Westview softcover editions are manufactured on our own premises using the highest quality materials. They are printed on acid-free paper and bound into softcovers that carry the highest rating of NASTA in consultation with the AAP and the BMI.

All rights reserved. No part of this publication may be reproduced or transmitted in any form or by any means, electronic or mechanical, including photocopying, recording, or any information storage and retrieval system, without permission in writing from the publisher.

Copyright © 1984 by Westview Press, Inc.

Published in 1984 in the United States of America by Westview Press, Inc., 5500 Central Avenue, Boulder, Colorado 80301; Frederick A. Praeger, Publisher.

Library of Congress Catalog Card Number: 84-51551
ISBN: 0-8133-0114-9

Composition of this book was provided by the editors
Printed and bound in the United States of America

10   9   8   7   6   5   4   3   2   1

TABLE OF CONTENTS

PREFACE

The period 1972-82 can truly be called a decade of disruption. The efforts of the environmental movement of the late 60's and early 70's led to the creation of legislation and public agencies, in most industrial nations, designed to regulate and control the environmental consequences of economic activity. The energy crisis, beginning in 1973-4, stimulated the planning and construction of large scale energy resource development projects, an explosion of activity which found a confluence in time with an environmental movement that had broadened its concerns to include the social, economic and political impacts of development. By the 80's, no large scale resource development project could be undertaken without the preparation of an environmental, economic and social impact assessment. Today, the energy crisis has receded, economic activity is depressed and the pressure for large scale energy resource development has, at least for the time being, abated.

In spite of the economic depression which currently grips the major industrial countries of the western world and the recent decline in oil and gas prices following the collapse of the OPEC cartel, large scale resource development projects, including energy resources, continue to be an important feature of many national economies. Certain megaprojects, particularly those dealing with heavy oil, tar sands and shale oil refining, planned in the late seventies and early eighties, have been postponed due to declining oil prices. However, these promise to re-emerge, albeit with different scale and timing, when oil prices resume their upward march. Major energy resource projects involving coal and hydro electric facility construction are proceeding while large scale projects for the development of other resources are still being planned and implemented.

Large scale resource development projects have important implications—social, economic, environmental and political—for the communities and regions in which they occur. These projects typically lead to dramatic increases in the population of a region; existing communities may absorb population ten or fifteen times their original size while elsewhere entirely new towns may be created. These projects and the resultant population growth create a range of problems and opportunities for the host communities and regions.

In 1980, a group of scholars from four nations, Canada, Norway, the U.K. and the U.S.A., who were interested in various problems of community development in small towns, particularly those experiencing the intrusion of new economic development, came together in Madison, Wisconsin to discuss these interests. The group, comprised of economists, geographers, sociologists, planners and management scientists, quickly

ix

focussed its discussions on the special problems confronting small communities in proximity to the unprecedentedly large scale resource development projects, particularly energy-related, then underway in the four nations. The Madison discussions led to an agreement to hold an international conference on energy-resource communities in Bergen, Norway, in August of 1981.

The Bergen Seminar focussed largely on the theoretical issues and methodological problems involved in investigating a series of socio-economic impacts, associated with large scale energy resource development projects, on a cross-national, comparative basis. The papers contributed to the Bergen Seminar were published in *Energy Resource Communities* (1982).

The Bergen Seminar also defined the next step in the research agenda as the preparation of a series of papers each of which would offer a systematic review of the state of the art of research respecting a specific problem confronting energy resource communities. These state of the art surveys would deal with such problems as income distribution, local decision-making, housing and social change; significantly, the problem of plant shutdown was recognized as being an issue of increasing importance, and was included in the research agenda.

These state of the art survey papers were prepared during 1981-82 and presented at the Second International Conference on Energy Resource Communities held in Calgary and Edmonton, Alberta, Canada in June, 1982. The individual papers were given extensive discussion, subsequently revised and compiled for publication in this volume. Hopefully they will be useful to scholars and practitioners in government and industry concerned with the impacts of large-scale resource development. Hopefully, as well, they will encourage others to investigate these problems within an interdisciplinary and international comparative framework.

Finally, an important issue was raised and discussed at this conference, but does not appear as a paper in this volume. Dr. Arne Selvik, president of the Norwegian Institute of Industrial Economics, suggested that a common thread running through the process of energy resource development in all four nations was the role of the multi-national corporation. In particular, he suggested that the behaviour of the multi-nationals within the widely differing political, economic, social and legislative milieus of the four nations was an important and relatively neglected area of comparative research. We need to know more about the ways in which the multi-nationals respond to the different national contexts within which they operate. An important conclusion reached by the participants at the Calgary-Edmonton conference was that this topic should be given high priority on its research agenda and provide an organizing theme for a subsequent conference of the four nations group.

ACKNOWLEDGMENTS

We wish to express our appreciation and gratitude to the following organizations for the financial assistance which made possible the Four Nations Conference and the publication of the original papers presented in this volume: Government of Alberta, Departments of Housing and Public Works and Environment; The University of Calgary, Research Grants Committee and The Faculty of Environmental Design; The University of Alberta.

We also wish to acknowledge the editorial and manuscript preparation assistance of Janet Harper. Her energy, enthusiasm and commitment to deadlines did much to ensure the timely and efficient production of these papers.

Finally, our thanks to Dr. Terry White, Dean of Arts at the University of Alberta and to Mrs. Irene Neat and the Support Staff of the Faculty of Environmental Design at the University of Calgary for the myriad of tasks which they quietly and cheerfully undertook to ensure the success of the conference.

D.D.D.

J.W.G

New Resource Towns on Canada's Frontier:

Selected Contemporary Issues

Ira M. Robinson

Faculty of Environmental Design
University of Calgary

An important manifestation of contemporary settlement patterns, the world over, is the emergence of new towns in previously unpopulated areas, often deliberately planned (or pre-planned) and built from scratch to serve a multiplicity of purposes. A common type of new town found in remote areas is the Resource Town, usually created by fiat of a private company (but sometimes by a government agency) to house and service the employees of that company engaged in the exploitation and/or primary processing of natural resources. These towns today are found in all areas of the world.

The Canadian new town that has received perhaps the most publicity and attention is Kitimat, British Columbia. Built in 1953, Kitimat was acclaimed as "the first completely 21st Century 'New Town', completely new, completely modern, in North America" (Architectural Form, 1954). Kitimat is a complete new town, but it was not the first built in Canada. In fact, more than any other country, Canada is a land of new towns; a large number of resource towns have been built and still exist.

The bulk of Canada's population (around 90%) is concentrated in a narrow belt of arable land hugging the Canada-United States border. The major exploitable resources, however, are mainly located north of this populated belt. Whenever resource development has occurred, the

1

lack of settlement and consequent shortage of labour near the resource to be exploited have made it necessary to create wholly new townsites to attract workers from distant areas.

Resource towns have been a continuous feature of Canada's historical development, for in the various surges of expansion that have marked this country's history, activity on the frontier has often been the quickening element. The building of such towns in Canada was especially marked in the years following World War II, reflecting the accelerated development of natural resources which sparked this country's "economic boom" in the immediate post-war period. And, when natural resources were exploited in sparsely populated areas, the creation of new communities was the common settlement pattern.

Many of the earlier townsites died as the natural resources were exhausted or for economic reasons-they are now only of historical interest as ghost towns. But many survived and together with those built recently, there now exist many communities built to serve forest, mining, power and petroleum developments. Two researchers recently identified approximately one hundred such communities (Betz, 1980; McCann, n.d.); in the majority of cases, the same towns are identified by both authors.

Although not large in terms of population, they nevertheless play an important role in the nation's economy. They seem destined to be more significant in the future when economic expansion will continue to depend upon development of its latent natural resource wealth. Indeed, several such towns are currently being constructed and others are at the planning or discussion stage; e.g., Tumbler Ridge in northeast B.C. (coal) and Cold Lake, Alberta (heavy oil).

Similar types of new towns are being planned for other parts of the world. Thus, an examination of Canada's resource towns might reveal some lessons for the planning and building of future new towns in other countries contemplating similar ventures. The purpose of this paper is to outline some of the major contemporary issues and problems facing these towns and the various ways that have been used or proposed to deal with them.

New resource towns face most, if not all, of the problems common to any rapidly growing small centre, any new town and to any town based on a single industry-plus several of their own which derive from the special conditions under which they are built. In this paper, I shall focus on the special conditions and problems of these towns, with occasional reference to similarities with circumstances facing new towns and small towns in general.

The following is a "shopping list" of the special problems which confront resource towns in Canada:

1. Instability and, in many cases, impermanence-a fluctuating often boom or bust cycle of growth;

2. An unbalanced demographic structure (in both construction and operations phases);

3. Isolation-physical and psychological;

4. The provision and financing of affordable housing of different types and qualities and the financing of an adequate range of physical and social infrastructures;

5. The appropriate concepts and techniques to use in the physical planning of these towns, given their unique geographical locations, small size, uncertain future, etc.;

6. Social, ethnic and cultural problems;

7. Their governance: the allocation of responsibility for pre-planning, planning, financing, building and governance, among the different actors (company, local government, citizens, senior governments), and at different stages of a town's growth and development.

This paper will focus on only a few of these problems, specifically numbers 1, 2 and 4, which are interdependent and the most critical. The other problems are addressed elsewhere in this volume. Although the subtitle of this paper is "Contemporary Issues", the problems are not just "contemporary" in nature; they are issues that have always afflicted resource towns in Canada. Indeed, an underlying premise of this paper is that, despite many of the improvements made over the years in the planning, design, development and governance of these towns, the basic problems, especially instability and impermanence, remain.

Instability and Impermanence

The most pervasive problem facing resource towns is their instability or impermanence, in terms of both population and economic growth. They display widely-fluctuating growth patterns and, often, a boom and bust cycle of development. The primary reason is that they are dependent on a single industry or company engaged in resource extraction or processing activities; both are highly volatile in their production and employment levels. A resource town's fortunes ride (generally like a roller coaster) with those of the industry.

Fluctuations in growth occur during the construction period and operations stage of the resource activity and townsite. The initial fluctuations and rapid growth stem largely from the fact that resource towns must be built quickly from scratch; as such, their growth pattern possesses many of the features common to all new towns. Initially, rapid population growth attends the construction phase of development, with workers employed in activities associated with constructing the resource-based facility and the townsite itself. The construction time is usually from three to eight years. After construction, the population tends to decline to a level related to the permanent labour force required for the operation of the facility.

The fluctuation in population between the construction and operations stages raises a number of questions relative to the planning and provision of housing and urban infrastructure. Should the towns attempt to meet the infrastructure demands of the peak population and risk the existence of excess capacity at the end of the construction phase? Can temporary housing and infrastructure be built initially and later converted into permanent facilities? Or should towns plan the urban infrastructure for the long-run stable population, which could result in a substantial deterioration in the quality of the urban environment during the construction period? Or is there some optimal combination of post-construction idle capacity and construction-period deterioration of service?[1]

More critical to the continued development of resource communities is the fact that they typically experience limited growth or worse, continue to experience fluctuations in population size, even after the construction period. During the operations stage and the permanent development phase of the town, the requisite size of the permanent labour force has supposedly been reached and population growth stabilized. But, typically, many resource towns reached their permanent labour force size and peak populations (of only a few thousand or less) and then declined and expanded frequently over time. The unstable growth pattern experienced by many resource towns after the initial development boom period is over is indicated in Table I. The reasons for this unstable growth pattern are discussed below in the section on "Reasons".

As implied earlier, many resource towns never recovered from economic setbacks and were abandoned altogether. However, not all abandoned resource towns date back to the early 1900's; many were built since the 1940's. Indeed, it is estimated that at least 30 resource towns were abandoned just since the early 1960's (Betz, 1980). As recently as 1972 three pulp and paper towns, part of a larger group built early in this century, were threatened with complete abandonment: Ocean Falls, British Columbia; Temiskaming, Quebec; and Corner Brook, Newfoundland.

Provincial and federal governments periodically come under pressure to "rescue" towns whose major industries are declining. In the case of Ocean Falls, the Province purchased the town and pulp mill plant and

Table 1.

RESOURCE TOWNS IN CANADA- 1979 .

Province and Town	Date Est.	Economic Activity	Population			
			1951	1961	1971	1976
Alberta						
Blairmore	1917	coal mining	1,933	1,779	2,037	2,321
Devon	1949	petroleum and natural gas	842	1,418	1,468	2,786
Grande Cache	1966	coal mining	*	*	2,525	4,116
British Columbia						
Ocean Falls	1909	pulp/paper	2,825	3,056	4,215	985
Port Alice	1917	forestry	1,038	952	1,507	1,497
Sparwood (Uninc.)	1939	coal mining	125	295	2,154	4,050
Manitoba						
Lynn Lake	1951	copper/nickel	925	2,082	3,012	2,732
Thompson	1958	nickel mining	*	3,418	19,001	17,291
Newfoundland and Labrador						
Buchans	1926	lead/zinc	1,944	2,463	454	521
Labrador City	1960	iron ore	*	386	7,622	15,781
Ontario						
Atikokan	1945	iron mining	5,855	6.674	6.087	5,803
Herron Bay South	1938	logging	168	136	7	175 (1974)
Jamestown (Wawa)	1946	iron mining	527	4,040	4,577	4,272
Longlac	1938	pulp/logging	696	1,125	1,484	1,934
Quebec						
Belleterre	1942	gold mining	1,011	n.a.	614	535
Gatineau	1926	pulp/paper	5,771	13,002	22,321	n.a.
Normetal	1937	copper, zinc mining and milling	1,486	2,285	2,105	1,524

* Towns established after the Federal Census for the designated year was taken.
Source: Marga E. Betz, "Community Stability in Resource Towns: Problems and Potentials", unpublished, 1980, Calgary. Partial listing of original table.

created a Crown Corporation to administer the facilities. The case of Temiskaming is particularly interesting since it represents one of the first attempts at cooperative ownership in a resource industry (and its associated town), between management, the workers, the provincial government and townspeople.

But, as raised by Hodge (1973), how many of the other 18 or so pulp and paper mills that were built in the same period as Ocean Falls and Temiskaming will falter and die in the near future, dragging their communities down with them and creating a public demand for government "rescue" measures? Even if the efforts are successful in Ocean Falls and

Temiskaming, *can* the public and, more importantly, *should* the public, take on the costs of saving the others? The costs to the residents and to the provincial and local governments of deciding what to do with community infrastructure and facilities, as well as the unemployed workers, are enormous when a resource town dies and must be abandoned.

Reasons

Narrow Economic Base:

The underlying reason for the boom or bust pattern of growth typical of most resource towns is that they began as a one-industry, often one-company, town, and most of them remain so; they have not been able to diversify their economic base. It is serious enough that they are a one-industry town; worse, the resource based activity on which the industry depends is typically vulnerable to wide fluctuations in production and employment.

Towns whose economy is based on the extraction and processing of a natural resource are affected by fluctuations in international trade and monetary systems. The prices of primary resources and derivative products tend to fluctuate in response to forces such as technological change, discovery of a new supply source, labour unrest and industrial disputes, exchange rate variations and numerous other factors which influence international demand and supply. Price changes frequently result in large and sudden fluctuations in the incomes of the primary producers, their employees and suppliers. It follows that a town which depends heavily on a primary producer will experience similar variations in income, expenditure, employment, and tax revenues. Further, since this industry is the major, or only source of employment in the town, unemployed workers (and families) are usually forced to leave and seek employment elsewhere. Thus, population may decline.

Not only are resource towns dependent on external market forces, but the decisions affecting the future of their resource based industry are made externally. Changes in government policies with respect to the industry can lead to production cutbacks and shutdowns, even though the local products continue to be marketable. These factors all contribute to the volatility of resource based industries and their associated settlements (DREE, n.d., p. 2). In general, management decisions respecting resource based industry are made in the industrial heartland of Canada or even outside of Canada. This problem is aggravated when the industry is foreign owned or controlled which is often the case.[2] This implies that Canadian, let alone local, control over the fate of the town, is much more difficult if not impossible and often subject to the attitudes of foreign investors.

These variations and uncertainties respecting the health of a resource town's economy in turn make it a risky place for other private investment even on a small scale. Existing businesses are reluctant to expand and diversify or may do so only slowly, and new business activities are harder to attract and retain. Thus, the development of a diversified and expanding local economy, needed to contribute to a stable social and political environment and to help insulate the town from the external economic shocks, is both more difficult and problematic.

Another factor which contributes to retarded growth and lack of diversification in the local economy is the fact that many natural resources are finite and non-renewable. In these cases the lifetime and continuity of existence of the town itself are uncertain. Most of Canada's ghost towns were originally based on non-renewable resources and were unable to attract other industries or replace the dependence on the non-renewable resource when it expired.

High Labour Turnover:

Another reason for the fluctuating growth pattern of resource towns, even in their operations phase, is high labour turnover, a longstanding problem that the companies and provincial governments had hoped to minimize, or eliminate, in the new planned resource towns built since the 1950's. They assumed that an attractive physical environment in a planned "model town" would attract a more stable, family oriented labour force and that this would not only make the employees contented residents but also better and happier workers.

Though there appears to have been considerable improvement over the earlier years, turnover rates continue to remain high in resource towns. Moreover, the rates vary enormously by town and industry. Mac-Millan (1974) found the gross turnover rate (including all quits, discharges, layoffs and all hiring in a typical year) in 67 mining towns ranged from zero to 2,200%; the latter was found to be the exception rather than the rule. Other studies (MSUA Inventory Report, 1977; Matthiasson, 1971; Veit, 1978) covered a variety of resource towns and found average turnover rates from 80% to 200%. Bradbury (1980), in his study of British Columbia Instant Towns, found that labour turnover remained high throughout the 1960's and then, in some cases, climbed slightly in the early 1970's. Even Kitimat, one of the more successful of the planned resource towns, experienced relatively high turnover rates.

The reasons for such high rates of turnover in resource towns and the characteristics of those who leave have received considerable attention by researchers. It appears that many factors account for the high labour turnover, ranging from community-related aspects, work-related factors, and various personal reasons (Lucas, 1971; MacMillan, 1974; Veit, 1978; Bradbury, 1980).

While it is clear that any or all of these factors are relevant to employee turnover, the literature is not conclusive about which is the most important. As MacMillan (1974) and others have argued, considerably more research is required before the complex relationships between these factors and labour turnover are more clearly understood. However, it is clear that labour turnover is costly to all parties concerned. Further, when workers continually leave their jobs it negatively affects various aspects of community life, particularly in resource towns where turnover invariably means people leave the community and new workers and families continue to arrive. In short, labour turnover means community turnover which is disruptive to social networks and local decision making, and detracts from community self-determination and individual satisfaction (Wichern, 1971; Matthiasson, 1971). This constant migration creates ". . . the most serious threat to the reliability of resource towns" (Riffel, 1975, p. 38).

Limited Alternative Employment Opportunities:

Few resource towns have succeeded in attracting additional employment opportunities in basic industries, even when diversification was a goal of the town plan; some have, but usually fortuitously (e.g. tourism). Most resource towns remain dependent upon a single industry, and often a single company; there are few job opportunities outside the dominant industry or company. This poses enormous problems for the workers in these towns, and for persons contemplating moving to such towns.

In "ordinary" communities, if there is a downturn in one sector, the workers laid off can usually be absorbed by other sectors of the local economy or, at worst, in a nearby town or city. This allows the employees to continue to maintain residence. By contrast, in resource towns when the major employer cuts back or shuts down altogether, laid off employees (and their families) plus workers in the related service industries are usually forced to leave the town to seek employment; there are virtually no alternative employment opportunities available to absorb the unemployed workers. Moreover, due to the generally isolated location of resource towns, there are no nearby towns to commute to for employment.

Other negative consequences flow from the absence of alternative job opportunities in resource towns. Employers presently prefer married, family-oriented employees, including females, due to their reliability and much lower turnover rates. As the plans for these towns included provisions to attract families rather than single males, the demographic characteristics began slowly to change. The problem is, however, that there are very few jobs available for either single women or the wives of employees. Several community satisfaction surveys have shown that this factor is considered a serious disadvantage to living in resource communities (Veit, 1978, pp. V-XXXV; Northern British Columbia Task Force, 1977, p. 29; MSUA. Inventory Report, October 1976).

Jobs are also extremely scarce for the children of resource company workers. They usually have to leave town in order to find employment or to obtain special post-secondary training. This effectively drains off the very persons who might add productivity and continuity to the town. Clearly, the opportunities for alternative employment will change little in a single industry, resource based community, unless the economic base broadens and diversifies.

Small Size:

Another factor contributing to the instability of resource towns is their small size. The development of new towns everywhere has been plagued by difficulties in achieving a large population size, without substantial government intervention such as heavy subsidies and in some cases even "forced measures" (Robinson, 1973). New resource towns in Canada are no exception; indeed, they are even worse off in this regard. They are not large in terms of population, and they rarely reach their planned/ designed size. As noted previously, many quickly reached their present populations of only a few thousand or less and have rarely continued to grow substantially thereafter.

There are several reasons why these towns are small and are probably destined to remain so, unless alternative economic activities can be attracted to them.

- Resource industries tend to be highly capital-intensive and thus the size of the permanent workforce (or "basic workers") is generally small.
- Resource industries tend to generate only a limited employment "multiplier" effect; that is, induced local employment tends to be small. Indeed, much of the nonbasic employment generated by the basic resource industry occurs in distant urban areas, in head office cities or even in foreign cities (if the industry is foreign owned or controlled). The size of the permanent labour force associated with the resource industry is generally fixed for much of the life of the resource; this eliminates opportunity for growth in the service or tertiary sector of the local economy. In fact, once an equilibrium position has been reached in the resource operation, there is little likelihood of secondary multiplier effects being initiated in the town, so long as it continued to remain dependent on a single industry (McCann, n.d.).

- Limited employment opportunities for women and young people reduce the multiplier effect; the income base of the family or household is narrowed, in turn restricting growth of the service sector.
- Few resource towns to date have succeeded in attracting secondary manufacturing industries, which would bring in more basic workers and in turn induce more nonbasic employment.
- Because these towns tend to be isolated and in harsh climates, they are not attractive places to live.
- They remain small enclaves; they rarely serve as regional service centres for the surrounding region, which could result in more employment and population growth.

Being small and dependent on a single, highly volatile industry, resource towns are unable to withstand the external "shocks" which contribute to their instability and impermanence.

Problems Created

Instability and impermanence create a whole set of problems for the planners, local governments, senior governments, and the townspeople. First, the retarded development of the local private economy and fluctuations in the town's growth create special difficulties in the provision, planning and financing of overall physical development and various public sector activities. Recently, permanent and expensive community facilities have been provided, as if the town would be stable and permanent. In general, uncertainty respecting the rate, direction and stability of growth in the local economy and the resulting population effects makes it difficult to plan the nature and timing of land development, housing and physical infrastructure. Planning in advance of need is difficult enough under the best of circumstances; under the conditions of extreme uncertainty and variability in future population growth, and thus of future public sector revenues, efficient financing of public works is most difficult.

Population and employment forecasts for resource towns have proved to be notoriously inaccurate. Rarely have any of the towns achieved the size originally forecast or planned, at least in the time periods anticipated. Yet, the initial infrastructure services were often planned and provided with the larger forecasted population in mind. In the case of Kitimat, for example, infrastructure was provided for 35,000 to 50,000 people; a smaller population and the subsequent limited revenue from a smaller tax base created a burden on the town, especially in the early years of its existence. In a few instances, notably Fort McMurray, Alberta, the opposite forecasting error occurred; the company consistently under-estimated the size of the permanent labour force.[3] As a consequence, total population increase was continuously being underestimated (Parkinson and Detomasi, 1980) until recently when tar sands developments began to slow down. This resulted in problems of under-extension; the town was continually trying to keep up with the demand for utilities, housing and community facilities.

The continuing fluctuations in population growth create substantial costs, both individual and social, for all concerned (see Betz, 1980). Further, if the town is actually abandoned, the value of its permanent facilities and infrastructure are lost; houses, community centres, utilities, etc., will have to be duplicated elsewhere for the out-migrants.

Possible Solutions

The obvious solution to the problem of instability and impermanence is the diversification of the local economy. As noted earlier, some towns, mainly fortuitously, have succeeded in attracting other economic activities (e.g. tourism), but this has been rare. Unlike most "ordinary" communities, resource towns are not able to diversify "automatically"; there are built-in obstacles to diversification which can only be overcome, if at all, by public policy and action.

Where the potential for economic diversification is very limited and especially where finite and non-renewable resources are to be exploited- or where the required public subsidies to attract new industries are deemed too expensive-several questions arise regarding the appropriate policy toward the building of resource towns in the future:

- Should we build new resource towns, as if they will be stable and permanent, knowing from experience that most of them, especially those built around a non-renewable resource, will ultimately have to be abandoned? Should decision-makers (the resource company and the relevant government) plan and provide the physical infrastructure needed for the development of the residences and commercial activities of a stable community? Should provincial government departments assist in the planning, design and financing of such developments?

- Alternatively, should development be "quick and dirty" and minimal, even "temporary" in nature, abandoning the possibility of creating an attractive, viable and stable community? And what should be done in the case of a town based on a non-renewable resource but where there might be a potential for a community to emerge and develop some sense of stability? What life expectancy of the major non-renewable resource-based industry is necessary for the creation of a permanent new town?

- Should alternative locations be selected which might have a greater potential for broadening the long term economic base of the resource town, but which might involve higher transportation costs (e.g. for commuters) in order to ensure survival of the town.

There are no easy answers to these questions but such questions have led some people to propose that in the future we should not create or facilitate the development of permanent communities especially where single or non-renewable resources are to be exploited. As the costs of providing physical infrastructure and social services have risen relative to transportation costs, the notion of a "No town" (Detomasi, 1979) as opposed to "New town" has been increasingly proposed for the exploitation of remote non-renewable resources or when, for whatever reason, long-term community viability appears limited. Analogous models to the portable town (based on the familiar trailer camp) were first proposed by Parker (1960) and later discussed by Robinson (1962). Also, a modern version of the dormitory work camp with weekly or biweekly migration of employees by air from existing urban settlements has been proposed as an appropriate response to finite resource and limited community lifetimes. Even the daily migration of the work force from a centrally located regional centre by means of high speed buses or trains is being increasingly advocated and adopted (Robinson, 1979).

These various "No town" options require further research to determine which are the most feasible. Some of the questions which need further study are: what would be the social and psychological impacts on the family of the husband/breadwinner being away so frequently throughout the year? Would single-parent (especially female) resource workers be able to make the required special arrangements for child care while they are living temporarily at the resource site? Recent forecast shortages of skilled male workers indicates a need for more female workers in this industry.

Unbalanced Demographic Structures

Since the late 1950's, those responsible for planning, building and developing resource towns have recognized the need to attract a more permanent family-oriented labour force and a generally more representative demographic structure in order to overcome the high labour turnover and social instability of the typical male-dominated and transient resource town of the past. The resource companies, encouraged by provincial governments, have come to realize that to attract permanent workers they must offer, in addition to high wages, good housing, schools, recreation facilities and other urban-type amenities for the wives and children in particular, and more democratic forms of local government. Have they been successful in these efforts? Is the demographic structure of these towns more representative of the general population? To answer this, it is useful to distinguish between the construction and initial operation stages and the permanent development stage of a town's development.

Construction and Initial Operations Stages

The workers employed initially in surveying, building roads and constructing the industrial plant and townsite are mostly single men. There are few women, single or married. Later, as industrial operations begin and as families migrate in, more women appear in the population; males continue to outnumber females even after the initial phase of a resource town's development. Also, during the initial operations and development phase, immigrants are young and mobile, typically between 20 and 40 years of age and (if married) have families that are larger than the Canadian average (McCann, n.d., p. 37; Bradbury, 1980, p. 30).

As noted earlier, the population of the resource town during the construction period is larger than it is once the permanent operations stages of the industry begin, and this creates a difficult problem of planning and providing services and facilities. This problem is further complicated since the characteristics of the population during the construction period are so different from those of the permanent phase labour force. Young, single, transient men require different and fewer services than females or families. The latter require family-oriented businesses and activities generally associated with a rich community life and a broader economic base. Many businesses and services are not generally required in the initial commercial or public service structure of the town but are needed by the sex and family structure which emerges later.

These problems have led Pressman (1978, p. 61) to recommend that construction workers might be recruited initially according to their demographic characteristics and willingness to settle in the town, including the possibility of undergoing retraining to fit their skills to its occupational structure. Pressman recognizes certain inducements would be required to encourage construction workers to commit themselves to remain in the permanent town.

Operations and Permanent Development Stage

While the unbalanced age, sex and family structure during the early years is largely expected, those responsible for planning and building resource towns have assumed that, as the permanent labour force settled in and as the towns "matured," the structure would become more balanced. Have the expectations been realized?

Table 2 compares a selected set of 1976 demographic indicators for a representative group of resource towns and a group of "typical"

Table 2

Demographic Indicators for Selected Resource Towns and Urban Municipalities, 1976

City / Town	Date established	Sex Ratio (Males/100 Females)	% School-age Children (Age 5-14)	Teenagers (Age 15-19)	% Persons 65 years and over	Median Age (years)
Resource Towns						
Glace Bay (N.S.)	n.a.	99	15.2	11.0	15.2	27.2
Labrador City (Nfld.)	1960	115	20.3	8.6	0.7	21.9
Port Cartier (P.Q.)	1959	107	59.1	11.8	1.8	23.0
Sheffervill (P.Q.)	1954	120	20.4	9.3	0.7	n.a.
Elliot Lake (Ont.)	1954	109	23.3	13.4	2.6	23.1
Kapuskasing (Ont.)	1921	106	20.8	11.9	6.5	24.7
Flin Flon (Man.)	1929	103	16.9	9.4	8.3	27.2
Fort McMurray (Alta.)	1964*	109	16.4	10.4	0.8	—
Kitimat (B.C.)	1953	111	21.5	11.0	1.2	24.1
MacKenzie (B.C.)	1966	119	23.5	11.1	0.6	21.8
Port Alice (B.C.)	1917	141	19.0	10.3	0.6	n.a.
Other Cities						
Oakville (Ont.)	—	100	20.1	10.7	5.5	n.a.
Swift Current (Sask.)	—	93	16.5	10.6	2.7	n.a.
Cranbrook (B.C.)	—	101	20.5	10.9	6.3	n.a.
Prince George (B.C.)	—	105	21.7	10.2	14.0	n.a.
Medicine Hat (Alta.)	—	99	16.5	10.4	6.3	n.a.
CANADA, all municipal cities, 5,000 and over	—	97	17.4	10.0	8.6	28.3

Source: 1976 Census of Canada
* Date when Tar Sands Development started in Northern Alberta. Fort McMurray had existed many years before that as a tiny hamlet.

municipalities in Canada, and the average of all Canadian municipalities of 5,000 persons and over. Table 3 compares the sex ratios in selected British Columbia resource towns for 1971 and 1976.

Table 2 shows that all of the resource towns listed, except for Glace Bay, have sex ratios greater than 100, compared with the Canada-wide average of 97 males for 100 females. In general, the data indicate that the older resource communities (e.g. Glace Bay) tend to have more equal sex ratios than the younger ones (Fort McMurray); this seems to confirm the expectations of the planners of these towns, and of researchers such as Riffel (1975) and Lucas (1971) who have hypothesized that such a change would occur.

Moreover, as can be seen in Table 3, the degree of sex imbalance, except in one instance, decreased somewhat from 1971 to 1976. However, in all instances, the sex ratio was higher than the average for all urban areas in British Columbia, excluding Vancouver and Victoria. This is true even for those "instant" resource towns based on older existing settlements (Port Alice, Sparwood) which continue to have high male sex ratios.

Table 3

Sex Ratios (*) in selected British Columbia Resource Towns, 1971 and 1976		
	1971 (a)	1976 (b)
Fraser Lake	129	118
Houston	118	122
Kitimat	116	111
Mackenzie	124	119
Ocean Falls	156	n.a.
Port Alice	153	141
Port Hardy	118	108
Sparwood	119	115
Stewart	125	n.a.
Tahsis	180	152
Trail	125	100
Ucleulet	129	118
All British Columbia municipalities (excluding Vancouver and Victoria)		
	110	99

* Number of males per 100 females.
Source: (a) J. Bradbury "Instant Resource Towns Policy in British Columbia, 1965-72, *Plan Canada*, Vol. 20, No. 1 (March 1980) p. 30. (b) Statistics Canada, Edmonton Office.

As discussed earlier, women in resource towns - single or married - have few employment opportunities. Equally important, the relatively small proportion of single females does not encourage long stays by younger men and, most importantly perhaps, a male-dominated demographic structure does not contribute to community stability or personal satisfaction (Bradbury, 1980, pp. 31-32).

Compared with other Canadian urban municipalities, resource towns have a much higher proportion of school aged children and young teenagers. This indicates that the policy of attempting to attract families to resource towns has succeeded to some extent.

In general, resource towns continue to be dominated by young people, even those towns that have existed for 20 or more years. The median age of all Canadian urban municipalities of 5,000 and over in 1976 was 28.3 years. For the towns listed in Table 2, the median age ranged from a low of 21.8 to 27.2; in short, there are few old people (see Table 2, column 4). However, as expected, the older communities (e.g. Glace Bay) have a larger proportion of "senior citizens".

Thus, despite the improvements, resource towns continue to attract a high proportion of young, single males and transients in general. This has important implications for the development of the private economy and for public policy as well. Clearly, the variety and quality of goods and services required by a population with these characteristics, will differ from that required for a more representative population structure. Also, clearly, developments which emphasize the needs of this particular group will make it more difficult to attract a more representative population to the town. The transient nature of the population (in many cases, fewer than 10% remain two or more years) means that, in the absence of effective public policy, it could take 10 or more years, if ever, for a town to develop a "critical mass of long term residents committed to the community and its future" (Detomasi, 1979, p. 141). Such a mass is necessary if the town is to attract the type of new residents needed for stable development and long-run survival.

There are two other sets of special problems faced by resource towns that I have identified as being critical - the provision and financing of housing and the provision and financing of physical infrastructure and social services. I will only briefly describe these as they are addressed more fully in Detomasi's paper.

Provision of Housing

Housing in resource towns serves other values, goals and needs in addition to shelter. Among the values and goals and special needs which housing should try to fulfill are the following:

1. Housing design is important to resident satisfaction and commitment to a resource community;

2. Long winters, harsh climate and limited recreational opportunities common to northern communities emphasize the house as a shelter and as locus for domestic and leisure activities;

3. A 24-hour work-shift in the major plants means that workers are on night shift a good part of the year and thus require more quiet and privacy in the dwelling during the day;

4. A concern for energy conservation requires greater attention to this in housing and sub-division design;

5. Housing is a means of getting people more involved in and committed to the town, e.g. through alternative tenures and self-help building practices;

6. Finally, and perhaps most important, housing is an incentive to attract and maintain a stable population.

In the effort to respond to the above, there are a number of problems which must be faced in providing housing in northern resource towns. Here I will deal only with the provision of appropriate types and variety of housing. (However, see Detomasi in this volume.)

Type and Variety of Housing

All previous surveys indicate that the aspirations of the majority of residents of resource towns are for single-family, detached housing (Matthiasson, 1971; M.S.U.A. study, 1977). A recent study of five Western Canadian Resource Towns found that between 92 and 99% of the residents indicated single family detached housing as their first preference (Praxis, 1982). Also, this form is believed to provide workers the greatest quiet and privacy during day-time sleeping hours. This housing preference creates a dilemma for those responsible for planning resource towns.

First, the evidence is that many Canadians cannot afford singlefamily detached housing today, at least as a first home. In northern resource towns housing is more expensive than in southern Canada, largely due to the high cost of construction.

Second, single family housing is not energy-efficient; as a building type it consumes more energy than higher-density units and it requires greater use of cars.

Thus far, this preference for single family housing has been largely satisfied, mainly through rental and purchase agreements involving some form of subsidy from the company. Whether companies will continue this in the future is problematical. Other approaches which deserve consideration-self-help building programs, different forms of tenure (e.g. co-op housing)[4] and innovative housing forms-would have several advantages; among them, cost reduction.

Choice of a variety of housing types to suit the diverse needs and lifestyles of resource town residents is often constrained by a number of forces. In particular, the small market makes it difficult for builders and developers to meet these diverse needs. In general, families are offered little choice but to occupy finished, standard-type houses, which do not necessarily fit their needs and lifestyles, and are not adaptable to their changing needs. This militates against development of resident involvement in the community and contributes to community instability. Greater self-involvement in providing housing should promote commitment to the town and reinforce stability.

In most cases housing in resource towns is basically southern housing transplanted to the northern environment (Robinson, 1962). All such housing seems to have initially met the original expectations of the residents, who clearly are conditioned by aspirations they bring with them. While there are a few examples of higher-density innovative housing forms (e.g. in Leaf Rapids, Manitoba and Fermont, Quebec), it is not certain that residents will be receptive to unfamiliar housing forms (Porteous, 1974). This is clearly a problem of educating residents to different housing options.

FINANCING AND PROVISION OF PHYSICAL INFRASTRUCTURE AND SERVICES

In order for resource towns to be successful in attracting a population which is less transient and more representative of the population as a whole in terms of age, sex, and family characteristics, they must provide a range of public and private goods and services which comprise an important element in the lifestyle of the typical family. In particular, this means a greater choice of outlet and diversity in the range of both consumption goods and consumer durable goods[5] and of personal services and community facilities than traditionally provided by the private and public sectors.

The provision of these goods, services and opportunities is much more difficult and expensive to achieve in a new town in a remote setting than it is in existing small towns, where at least some of these requirements are already being met. Indeed, the cost to governments (local and senior) of providing the necessary physical infrastructure and facilities and the required range of social services, coupled with the initial subsidies required to attract diverse private sector activities, may simply be too heavy to be justified, except in the case of very large resource development projects, with associated large long-lived resource towns, such as Thompson, Manitoba (Detomasi, 1979, p. 142). For this reason alone there are many cases where a "no town" may be the optimal solution.

Thus, many potential new resource towns are confronted with a chicken-egg proposition: on the one hand, they wish to attract a population comprised mainly of young families who will stay and help build the community; on the other, they cannot attract this population unless they are able to provide a wide range of both public and private goods and services, the availability and provision of which, in turn, usually requires the prior existence of the population. Provision of facilities and services in advance of need is a risky business, particularly for small private businesses- the desired population may just not come. Thus, financing this range of services, both the front-end capital and operating costs, plus the town's share of the costs associated with the provision of physical infrastructure, constitute major problems.

However, chances have to be taken. The resource companies and local and provincial governments have a vital stake in the stable long-term development of these towns. New ways should be sought in which they both individually and cooperatively can expand the range of goods, services and opportunities available to existing and potential residents.

These problems- ensuring the provision of satisfactory housing, attracting a diverse family-oriented population (making the community more attractive to women) and financing the provision of an expanded range of physical facilities and social services — are all highly interdependent. In turn, they are related to the first problem discussed in this paper- the need to diversify the local economic base. The achievement of one of these objectives tends to have positive effects on the others and the achievement of any one depends, in part, on the realization of the others.

If the resource town, with the support of various provincial and federal government programs, is successful in attracting new economic activity and in creating an environment for the expansion of existing activity, three important consequences should follow: first, a basis is laid which makes further economic diversification and expansion more likely and less difficult, including the attraction of the necessary retail and personal services. Second, such expansion and diversification increases the number and variety of employment opportunities resulting in a larger and more diverse total population. Third, the expansion of local economic activity contributes to an increase in tax assessments, both through increases in land values and through property improvements.

Similarly, if the major employer and local government, assisted by senior governments, are successful in creating a range of housing types and qualities at affordable prices and in providing the range of physical facilities and social services required, a number of other desirable consequences should follow. First, appropriate housing and supporting physical and social infrastructure will make the community an attractive place in which to live, contributing to the goal of attracting a more representative, family-oriented population to the town. Second, the activities needed to produce an adequate housing stock contribute to the diversification of the supply and service sector of the local economy, increasing employment and expanding its economic base. Third, these additions to the housing stock of the community contribute to a significant increase in the property tax assessments. This increase and the new assessments generated in the commercial and/or industrial sectors should increase the town's ability to finance the physical infrastructure and the social services required by an éxpanded and more demographically representative population.

Nevertheless, resource towns are still apt to find themselves in a financial "squeeze". Typically, increases in tax assessments, especially in small towns faced with sudden growth, are not sufficient to finance substantial increases in physical infrastructure and social services. This is especially true if population increases begin to exceed a threshold at which it becomes necessary to invest in major upgrading and/or resizing of major infrastructure utilities such as sewage treatment facilities. Even with provincial grants, the resource town may incur relatively large capital expenditures which must be spread over a rapidly growing, but still relatively small population. This could result in high per capita debt. In short, the experience of small towns, including resource towns, is that population growth generates higher public expenditures than the property tax revenues derived from such growth.

Yet, despite this financial squeeze, these expenditures on physical infrastructure and social services and facilities are absolutely necessary if remote, resource-based towns are to achieve their objectives of creating a stable, demographically varied population and of diversifying the local economy. To achieve this requires new avenues of cooperation and cost sharing among local governments, citizen's groups and the resource companies; this seems more likely today than in the past, particularly because the companies appear to share these objectives. Similarly, senior government programs of financial assistance, especially federal, should be expanded.

CONCLUSIONS

In conclusion, what can be said about the building of future towns in connection with resource developments which might take place in unpopulated areas? I believe that realization of the objectives discussed in this paper- a more balanced demographic structure, an adequate supply of affordable housing of different types and qualities, financing physical infrastructure and other required personal and business services and, above all, achieving community stability and permanence- will depend, first on a careful assessment (by senior governments and the resource companies themselves), of the potential of each prospective town to become a stable and permanent "new town"; and, second, on the willingness of the parties to invest the necessary financial and other resources to realize these potentials. (If there is limited potential for a long-life, a "no town" solution should be adopted.) This, in turn, should have a positive effect on the attitudes of prospective residents towards these towns as permanent places in which to live, give birth, work, shop, recreate, retire and ultimately die. The latter attitude is most important, for as the history of cities the world over has demonstrated, where people desire to be buried is often the best indicator of what they consider their permanent hometown to be.

Notes

1. See Cummings and Mehr, 1977, for a proposal as to how to determine an optimal investment strategy for investments in urban infrastructure in boom towns.

2. While there is little documentation on the corporate linkages between resource towns and foreign companies, Bradbury (1980, p. 22) found that eight out of ten resource communities established during the 1960's were dependent on foreign owned corporations.

3. Unlike conventional oil processing, these plants are relatively labour labour-intensive. For example, in October, 1978, the Suncor Operations workforce was 1500 and Syncrude's was 3,000. See Parkinson and Detomasi (1980).

4. An Urban and Regional Planning student in the Faculty of Environmental Design is investigating, under my guidance, the potential feasibility of co-op housing as a means of minimizing labour and community turnover and achieving greater community stability in resource towns.

5. Most surveys of resident satisfaction in resource towns indicate that the number one complaint of the majority of residents is with the limited range of retail outlets, including food stores (and the high prices charged therein) and of personal services, eg. lawyers, dentists, psychiatrists.

Decision-Making Under Uncertainty:

Public Facilities and Services
Provision in Energy Resource Communities

Kristi M. Branch
Douglas A. Hooper
James R. Moore

Mountain West Research-North, Inc.
Billings, Montana

1. INTRODUCTION

It is well-recognized that the provision of adequate public facilities and services is socially, economically and politically important to both the decision-makers and residents of communities. Indeed, this constitutes the major concern of most community decision-makers. Adequate service provision is problematic even under optimal conditions. The difficulties are greatly increased when, as in many energy resource communities, demand fluctuates widely in both volume and kind, and the decisions regarding service provision are made in an environment of uncertainty. The combination of changing demand and uncertainty has profound effects on decisions in rural energy resource communities.

The purpose of this paper is to examine service provision as a complex decision-making process and to consider how it is affected by the changes in demand, resources and the uncertainty associated with energy resource development. Initially, the analysis focuses on small, rural communities in the western U.S. where the pregrowth service provision process is well-established, if limited. A framework is then developed to examine the effects of energy development on the service provision process in company towns and in other countries–e.g., Norway and Canada–where the roles of governments and companies are quite different.

The paper is organized into four sections. Section two describes the service provision process employed in the western United States. Section

23

three identifies the problems that energy resource development creates for small, rural communities with existing service provision systems and some of the major sources of uncertainty for local decision-makers. Section four discusses the mechanisms that have been developed to address the problems and to cope with the uncertainty. Section five discusses the major conclusions and raises the possibility of applying this analysis to company towns and to communities in other countries.

To date, little attention has been paid to these aspects of community service provision. Instead, the analysis has generally been at a relatively low level, focusing upon the establishment of service standards (Murdock and Leistritz, 1979; Leistritz and Murdock, 1981) or on methods to finance new or expanded services (Barrows and Charlier, 1980; Murray, 1980). Few analyses consider the provision of services as a decision-making process that occurs in an environment of uncertainty influenced by historical patterns, expectations and concerns.

2. COMMUNITY SERVICE PROVISION AS A DECISION-MAKING PROCESS

In most communities in the United States, the provision of facilities and services–or community services–constitutes the major direct and indirect function of government. Although the specific responsibilities vary, direct responsibilities generally include the provision and maintenance of streets and roads, schools and educational services, water and sewer systems, health facilities, welfare services, parks and recreation programs. Indirect responsibilities often include regulatory or control functions such as zoning, utility regulation, user fees, etc. (Hitzhusen and Napier, 1978).

In addition to meeting the service needs of community residents, community services also provide integrative mechanisms for the community (Rogers and Pendleton, 1978; Rein, 1980) and an opportunity for expression of local democratic control. Both directly and indirectly, community service provision influences the overall social organization of the community. Community services are also important to overall resident satisfaction with community life (Molnar, 1979; Dillman and Tremblay, 1974; Marans and Rodgers, 1975).

To understand the effects of energy resource development on decision-makers and community services in the small, rural communities, it is necessary to understand some of the distinctive characteristics of these communities. It is important to appreciate the complexity of the decision-making process by which community services are provided. Decisions that affect community services are made by a wide range of community residents and by far distant individuals and organizations

(Warner, 1974; Warner, 1978; Bradshaw and Blakely, 1979). Through this complex process decision-makers respond to the demands of community residents. Thus, the provision of community services in rural communities experiencing energy resource development must be seen not simply as a problem of meeting service standards or of obtaining necessary revenues, but as a complex and time-consuming process involving the community and an ever-widening and diverse environment. Even in small rural communities, service provision is the result of many inter-linked decisions, many of which are made by persons not directly responsible for the service itself.

Many energy resource communities in the western United States were small and isolated, and had experienced out-migration and population decline prior to energy development. Historical and ecological conditions encourage individualism and independence and a distrust of senior government intervention in local affairs. With limited economies and tax bases and a declining population, decision-makers and residents were generally acutely aware of the tension between service provision and revenues. Differences in economic interests and the distance of rural residents from the towns frequently led to conflict/disagreement between counties and towns–the two levels of government responsible for community services provision. Nevertheless, because change was usually gradual and predictable, the level of public facilities and services in many of these communities came to represent an equilibrium between service priorities and a desire for lower taxes.

In these communities, public services were often limited; community leaders were reluctant to undertake new projects and restricted themselves to "housekeeping" activities (Vidich and Bensman, 1968). They employed a balanced budget and followed conservative fiscal policies; existing facilities, personnel, legislative structure and tax bases were maintained at levels which provided little excess capacity for the absorption of growth. In many communities, public officials served voluntarily; most had little or no experience with growth or rapid change.

It was generally in or near these small, western communities that the rapid energy growth of the 1960s and 1970s occurred, and it was to these decision-makers and community residents that the magnitude and implications of the uncertainties associated with energy development were made evident. The importance of this process and the difficulties posed by resource development have made community service provision the focus of much concern and negotiation regarding responsibilities and strategies for controlling the impacts of development. The full implications of energy resource development for local decision-makers and community service providers and the identification of effective mechanisms of response are best approached by viewing community services provision as a dynamic process that is itself affected by the efforts to respond.

3. THE PROBLEMS POSED BY ENERGY RESOURCE DEVELOPMENT

The following section discusses the nature of the environmental uncertainty in which socioeconomic decisions must be made and identifies some of the problems energy development creates for local decision-makers in the western United States.

3.1 The Definition of Environmental Uncertainty

Environmental uncertainty occurs when the environment of an organization or community increases in complexity and number of interrelationships (Duncan, 1948). Lablebici and Salancik (1981) suggest that this type of uncertainty can cause roles and responsibilities to become unclear and unfamiliar. When it is extreme, the relationships among alternatives is so obscured that decision-makers have difficulty determining what information they need to make a decision or to evaluate alternatives. Decision-makers in communities experiencing large-scale energy development face two types of environmental uncertainty. The first derives from the characteristics of energy resource development and its effects on service demand. The second derives from the changes in the decision-making process itself.

3.2 Changes in Demand for Services

Decision-makers are faced with two essential problems: (1) determining the magnitude and characteristics of future service demand and (2) making the necessary services available without providing more capacity than is needed. The characteristics of energy resource development and its accompanying service demands make these problems extremely difficult to solve. These projects are known for their unpredictability. Projects are announced which never occur. Projects are started and then cancelled or dramatically altered in schedule or scope. Information about project (and demand) characteristics is unreliable and difficult to obtain.

Local socioeconomic impacts from energy resource development result from direct, indirect and induced employment, income and population changes generated by a project's hiring and local purchasing actions, as well as by its expansion of the local tax base. Energy resource developments are typically large-scale, multiyear projects whose employment and assessed valuation come to dominate local conditions. They have several characteristics which affect the service provision process.

First, as shown dramatically by their recent performance, they are volatile and subject to unpredictable fluctuations as world market conditions and governmental policies change. Second, in addition to, and aggravating this basic volatility, these activities typically exhibit cyclical fluctuations in work force requirements that correspond to three major project phases–construction, operations and shutdown. Furthermore, because they are based on nonrenewable resources, many projects have a predetermined, generally limited, operating lifetime. Third, communities often face impact from several projects at once, many based on the same energy resource and dependent upon similar economic conditions for viability. Consequently, the number of actors and the uncertainties are often multiplied.

As shown in Figure 1, the natural cycle of energy resource development causes local employment to expand rapidly, reach a peak and then decline rapidly to an operations level which persists for a finite period before undergoing rapid decline at shutdown. If local labor is inadequate (in number, skills, and/or union affiliation) to fill the employment opportunities created by the project, in-migration of workers and families occurs. This in-migration causes population to grow and increases facility/services demands. If the in-migrating population is significantly different from the existing population in demographic characteristics or service preferences, shifts in service demand disproportionate to the change in population size can result. Regardless of whether local residents or in-migrants are employed on the project, the fluctuations in employment shown in Figure 1 mean unstable population and income in the community and fluctuations in service demand and available tax base.

The specific nature of the demands for community services also depends on the conditions that prevail in the community over time. For example, conflict among newcomers or between newcomers and longtime residents may increase demands for law enforcement, judicial personnel, etc. Shortages in housing or utilities can increase the need for family counselling services–or it may discourage in-migration.

In many energy resource communities, the changes in service demand are so large, rapid and wide-ranging that they affect all aspects of service provision. Response to such dramatic shifts often requires profound changes in the organizational structure of the community and its decision-making processes. Because these changes are interlinked, happen quickly, and are driven by highly variable and uncertain factors, they are particularly difficult to handle, making the decision-making context in resource communities unusually pressured and turbulent. These problems are exacerbated by the characteristics of the existing systems, described in section 2, and the required changes in organizational structure and decision-making processes.

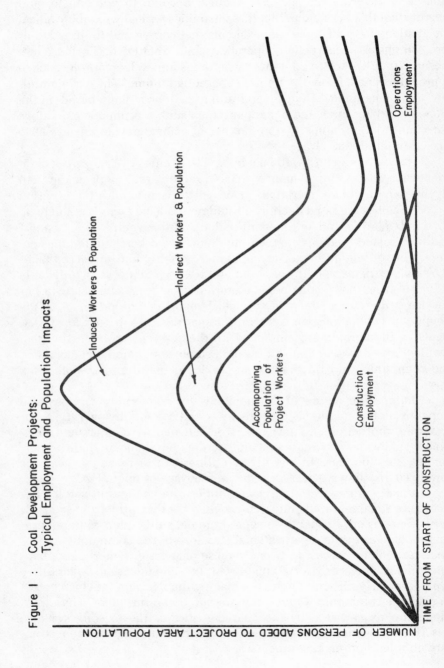

Figure 1 :   Coal Development Projects:
Typical Employment and Population Impacts

3.3 Changes in Organizational Structure and the Decision-making Process

In western communities facing large-scale development, established priorities–and hence the equilibrium between demands and resources that has been created–tend to be disrupted as large numbers of new residents and resources appear. The organizational context is quickly transformed from one where priorities are well established, widely accepted by residents and understood by decision-makers, to one where priorities are unclear, substantial differences exist among residents, and the political consequences of decisions are uncertain. In addition, decision-makers must simultaneously manage an ever-widening, complex and unfamiliar network of relationships and communication/negotiation procedures that are neither stable nor well established. This transformation and the uncertainties it introduces is often difficult for decision-makers to deal with, particularly if there is dissent or conflict.

The most important changes in organizational structure and the decision-making process that affect community service provision include:

1) Changes in the assumptions about and mechanisms for delineating services provision responsibility.

2) Changes in the complexity and linkages of the decision-making process.

3) An increased need for formal structures and professionals.

4) Changes in the need for information.

5) Changes in the criteria for success.

Delineation of Responsibility

Prior to the 1970s, responsibility for community service provision clearly rested with the community in most areas. Furthermore, "the new federalism" shifted economic and administrative responsibility for an array of nationally mandated service functions to the states and municipalities. As large-scale projects were implemented throughout the West, it became evident that the magnitude and timing of that development created demands which were often beyond the capabilities of local governments. Serious inadequacies developed.[1] The resulting problems threatened to become roadblocks to further implementation of such projects. Since the location of the resource generally made it impossible for development companies and governmental agencies to shift development to more populous areas where service capacities were higher, considerable pressure arose to increase or supplement local capabilities, thus preventing serious service and facility inadequacies and reducing opposition to further development.

Companies and some governmental agencies were motivated by these considerations to expedite the provision of community services. Simultaneously, they sought to avoid unnecessary responsibility and expense. An increasingly elaborate analytic, forecasting (EIS), and negotiation process for allocating service provision responsibilities among corporate and government agencies emerged. Service provision was no longer unquestionably a local responsibility. Instead, socioeconomic assessments and the negotiating skill of community representatives became important factors in the allocation of responsibility.

Although these changes created opportunities for communities to obtain assistance, they also introduced unfamiliar procedures and introduced uncertainty to the decision-making process. A principal concern of community leaders and residents of energy resource communities in the West, in the reallocation of responsibilities, was to preserve control over facility and service decisions while obtaining funding assistance for program implementation. Their desire to maintain local control was based, in part, on the knowledge that responsibility for facilities and services would ultimately revert to the community.

Increased Complexity and Linkages

In the energy resource area of the western United States, local governments have been relatively isolated, with limited linkages to outside agencies and, frequently, little demonstrated ability to cooperate. Relationships between towns and counties and between school districts were often strained. The lack of mechanisms or habits of cooperation aggravated the problems of meeting rapidly changing, uncertain demand and constrained local decision-makers' ability to manage growth. In order to negotiate effectively or to provide necessary services, government and corporate decision-makers frequently needed to establish more extensive linkages and new patterns of cooperation. The new structures and legislative mechanisms that were developed increased the network of participants in the process, the interdependence and, sometimes, the sharing of responsibility among various jurisdictions.

Bradshaw and Blakely (1979) have noted that when rural areas are drawn into interdependent relationships, four important organizational changes occur which can cause environmental uncertainties:

1) Rural governments became more tied to larger and larger social units such as state and federal governments.

2) Rural governments require more steps to get things done and more complex paths of influence are developed.

3) Actions themselves become increasingly complicated, involving coordination and planning rather than simply a transfer of funds or provision of a service.

4) More complex issues require consideration over an increasingly long span of time (Bradshaw and Blakely, 1979).

Obviously, such changes expand the decision-making context and affect decision-making styles. For example, a community requiring a sewer system must meet not only local needs, but also complex and stringent state engineering standards, public health codes and Environmental Protection Agency guidelines and standards. Funding is likely to come not only from local revenues, but also from state and federal agencies. System capacity may be dictated by an outside agency that is using projections of the community population over which local residents have little influence. Interaction between these various actors differs from that of the traditional town-level meetings.

As the communities become more linked to the larger urban society, there are a greater number and variety of organizations and forces that rural decision-makers must consider as they govern their communities. The community service responses required by energy development increase the speed and extent of these changes. To be effective, local service providers are increasingly required to establish technical competence and political contacts outside the community and to coordinate an everwidening network of relationships.

A large-scale resource development creates a situation of potential environmental uncertainty for local decision-makers; they must quickly establish a set of relationships and an organizational structure while simultaneously making decisions affecting the interests of the community (and themselves). Because there are likely to be differences in objectives among the key participants, both with respect to desired roles and allocated responsibilities, the complexity of the interactions and the uncertainty of the outcome are substantially increased.

Increased Need for Formal Structures and
Professional Planners and Administrators

As interdependencies increase in number and complexity, local decision-makers must institute formal procedures, establish rules, hire professional staff, and allocate more time to dealing with project-related issues. In addition there are increased demands on time and skill required to plan and administer community services programs (MWRI, 1982). Frequently, this increased professionalism, formality, and interdependence constitutes a profound change in governmental organization. It can confuse or alienate longtime residents, place additional burdens on decision-makers, and increase the uncertainty of the decision-making context.

3.4 Changes in the Need for Information, Its Sources and Use

As communities move from an environment of relative stability to one of rapid change, information needs increase. This is especially true for decision-makers confronted by large-scale resource development. The particular influencing factors are the following:

1) Large-scale development frequently requires modification or expansion of all aspects of community service provision in a coordinated manner. Problems are not generally limited to one or two areas at a time.

2) The peak-decline pattern of population growth requires more careful planning and analysis than for a unidirectional trend.

3) The timing and exact nature of growth and demand are uncertain; they are known to be highly volatile and, in many cases, capable of being substantially altered by a single corporate decision.

4) The allocation of responsibility and magnitude of resources available for response are increasingly dependent upon negotiations rather than on preestablished criteria.[2]

Companies and regulatory agencies have responded to changing information needs by developing community service and fiscal analyses and forecasts and communities have hired professional administrators and planners. As the importance of public service provision became recognized, the analysis and forecasts became more detailed and sophisticated and acquired an increased role in environmental assessment. Forecasts of the effects of resource development on the availability and cost of community services, especially for local residents, were made. In some cases, the impact of community efforts to provide facilities and services on the characteristics of local government were assessed.

Although local decision-makers were generally consulted, control of both the process and information was seldom in their hands. From their perspective, this created two major problems. First, the forecasts and analyses were inaccessible because of their complexity, sponsorship, and cost. The forecasts frequently involved computerized models, required extensive data, and were time-consuming and expensive to construct. Even after the models had been developed, access to a computer terminal and some training was necessary to fully utilize the results. Local decision-makers rarely had the time, budget, or skills to participate fully in this process.

Second, even the most detailed forecasts were highly unreliable and, despite improvements that occurred during the 1970s, problems remained. The most significant were with the unreliability of the information upon which the forecasts were based, not with the analytical tools. Project descriptions and baseline conditions changed frequently and substantially; forecasts of revenues and expenditures depend on assumptions about project characteristics, statutes, allocation of responsibilities, and decision criteria that were too unpredictable to yield reliable forecasts (Moore, 1979). Moreover, the key economic factors underlying energy development have been highly unpredictable and volatile - particularly within the time frames required for community response to anticipated public facilities/services problems (Anonymous, 1982).

Despite these problems, the need for information for negotiating roles and responsibilities and for decisions regarding facility and service expansion gave such forecasts a strategic and political importance. In some ways, this increased rather than reduced the uncertainties facing decision-makers by providing unreliable but precise information to local decision-makers, state agencies and companies alike.

3.5 Changes in the Criteria for Success

While decision-makers in energy resource communities are being faced with the establishment of major linkages outside the community, they are often also faced with the potential for significant change in the organizational characteristics of the community itself. These changes create uncertainty at both a personal and professional level. As organizational characteristics change, new and different demands are placed on decision-makers. New skills and priorities are required. As decision-makers and participants in the community, community leaders often have a dilemma; whether to lead organizational change by pushing for more formal and technical methods and allowing new procedures to emerge, or to resist change by attempting to maintain the status quo.

The conditions created during resource development are often unique in the experience of the community and residents and decision-makers have difficulty forecasting the trade-offs they would make under these conditions. Examples of these trade-offs are: whether to suffer acute facility shortages for several years or to suffer higher taxes; whether to develop recreational facilities or expand medical facilities; whether to add staff to maintain existing staff ratios or to avoid the problems of large personnel cut-backs once the peak is past by increasing staff loads.

In addition, decision-makers become personally and politically vulnerable. Criteria for evaluation of decisions and performance become unclear. If plans are good and implementation solid, but the program fails because the expected population does not materialize, how are the decision-makers to be evaluated by the community or by themselves? If the population growth is so high that the best the community can hope to do is survive (and they do) unpleasantly, how should the decision-makers be evaluated? If it is not clear that the approach being taken is working, under conditions of rapid change in the community, how are decision-makers to know whether they should persist, or change tactics? Such questions increase the uncertainty and difficulties for local decision-makers.

4. MECHANISMS OF RESPONSE

Several mechanisms have been developed at state and local levels to mitigate energy development-related problems. Many focus specifically on reducing the uncertainty and risk for local decision-makers. Six types of "mitigation" mechanisms are discussed here:

1) Legislation and regulatory change
2) Planning and scheduling changes
3) Physical design
4) Program design
5) Organizational modification
6) Fiscal/financial strategies

4.1 Legislation and Regulatory Change

Several new laws were passed in the late 1970s by western states in the U.S.:

(1) industrial siting legislation which established permit processes for large industrial facilities (energy was the particular target) that enabled state and local governments to require project sponsors to assume some responsibility for impact mitigation,

(2) steeply increased severance taxes on mineral fuels which transferred funds from the resource developer (and consumer) to state and local governments,[3]

(3) modification of state laws to permit greater flexibility in taxation and bonding and in cooperation between local governments.

For example, the "Joint Powers Act" in Wyoming allows revenue-rich counties or school districts to join with revenue-poor towns in meeting the public service requirements of both.

Because local communities were recognized as disadvantaged in the struggle for roles and delegation of responsibility, numerous legislative actions were taken to structure this process, define roles, and provide guidelines for the allocation of responsibilities. NEPA and the state facility siting acts instituted in the mid-1970s are examples. Two key objectives of these initiatives were (1) to give local governments legislative mechanisms that increased their ability to affect the wider allocation of responsibility for providing services, and (2) to ensure that local government and residents had reasonable access to the information and analytic tools necessary to evaluate the effect of a project on the community and their lives.

The distribution of responsibility among affected communities in the western U.S. illustrates the variations in process and outcome of these negotiations. In some communities where local government was either very small or very limited in capability, corporations took major responsibility for service provision. Montana Power Company's activities in Colstrip, Montana is an example of this result. In other communities, revenues from state impact assistance funds reduced the financial need for a major company role. (Indeed, after 1975 most heavily impacted communities received state impact assistance funds.)[4]

During the most recent rounds of permit and siting applications in the western U.S., negotiation of corporate responsibility for service provision (and housing) has almost always been required by the state and local review process. Although impact assessments underlie many of these negotiations, the process remains highly political. Acquisition of local and state support for a process through which impact mitigation responsibility is allocated is a strategy frequently used by local decision-makers to increase the opportunities for success. The establishment of relationships between local governments and outsiders has become more structured and more predictable. Nevertheless, substantial uncertainties for local decision-makers and residents remain.

Regulatory requirements for the appropriate allocation of impact mitigation responsibility - particularly to the energy resource developer - have not been wholly restricted to the state and local permitting and review processes. Various federal agencies (e.g., the Office of Surface Mining or the Bureau of Land Management) have begun to grapple with committed mitigation actions by the applicant/energy developer as conditions of their leasing and mining permits. Of these agencies, OSM and BLM at present interpret their statutory authority to allow the inclusion of mitigation requirements in the permits granted.

4.2 Planning and Scheduling

Many small communities that experienced resource development during the 1970s were not accustomed to planning or scheduling service provision either at an agency or community-wide level. Many had experience with land use planning or regulation but, prior to their exposure to rapid, uncontrolled development, held it in low esteem. As the problems of controlling growth and providing public goods emerged, many communities instituted planning procedures, land use plans, zoning ordinances, subdivision regulations, and other controls. In order to avoid financing new services on the previous tax base, stiff utility hook-up charges and development requirements were frequently instituted.

In some communities, such efforts resulted in both controlled physical and financial growth. Risks of incompatible land uses were reduced, but not eliminated. Accommodations were made in the facilities and services infrastructure to meet the demands of population growth. It was in communities where the development uncertainties and burdens and local governmental limitations in capacity could not be overcome that the infamous "boomtown" characteristics were likely to develop.

4.3 Physical Design

The need to control cost and to provide temporary facilities during construction periods encouraged development of innovative infrastructure systems. Modular units or units that could be converted from temporary to permanent uses have been increasingly used by local planners and developers. Methods to temporarily expand sewage and water systems have been developed which satisfy peak demands without incurring long-term debt and operating costs. The use of construction camps, including units that could be disassembled and taken elsewhere, has been common. These approaches have limited long-term exposure to fixed debt burdens with a declining population and offered alternatives for more rapid response to facilities/services needs. Similar approaches were adopted for schools and recreation and health care facilities.

4.4 Program Design and Staffing

Efforts to address the problems residents experience during rapid growth and to accommodate the peak/decline pattern common in energy communities often leads to new programs or staffing arrangements. Some modifications are designed to serve multiple purposes, thus cutting the cost and administrative requirements of establishing several different programs. Others are designed to cover peak conditions through the use of special programs, scheduling, or staff patterns (e.g., increasing class sizes, double shifts) thus minimizing the need to expand facilities.

4.5 Social Organization

A major effect in a rapid growth community is the change in social organization as relationships change to accommodate new people and activities. The demands upon most governmental agencies increase dramatically with rapid growth and are aggravated by uncertainty. This has led community authorities to hire professional staff and/or to obtain technical skills themselves, and to increase the formal planning and administrative functions of service or governmental agencies. Further, since resource-generated growth often creates problems which require increased intergovernmental coordination, legislative and organizational changes have often been made, establishing joint planning commissions, councils or boards. A factor deterring local decision-makers in this respect is the loss of local control that accompanies the establishment of such legally empowered organizations.

4.6 Financial/Fiscal

A variety of fiscal/financial mechanisms have been developed to cope with the revenue requirements of rapid increases in the demand for public goods and to moderate the effects of uncertainty. Some of these mechanisms have resulted from legislative changes at the state level (e.g., changes in taxing or bonding authority). Others involve the implementation of existing legislation to facilitate flows between local jurisdictions (joint powers agreements) or between the jurisdiction and the energy companies. Loan guarantees, prepayment of taxes, industrial revenue bonds, and bond guarantees are among the mechanisms used by resource communities in the western U.S. to obtain funds and to spread the risk of expanding services for a larger projected population.[5] Several communities have further responded to the peak-valley and long-term high risk characteristics of resource development economies by shortening their bonding cycles to five years rather than twenty or thirty years, by imposing sales taxes during the peak years, and by adopting marginal cost pricing for facilities/services. In addition, by requiring energy companies to provide housing for their workers and to pay for increments to local public services, communities have avoided further costs. In Moon Lake, Colorado, for example, a substantial advance payment from the energy developer was negotiated by local governments to cover anticipated impacts of a coal-fired power plant.

5. MAJOR CONCLUSIONS

Based on the preceding analysis, it is evident that coping with uncertainty and managing risk is one of the major tasks of local decision-makers in western U.S. energy resource communities. Decision-makers in these communities live and work in an environment of economic and organizational uncertainty. The tentative nature of all projects, of all forecasts, of all indicators–of today's reality–makes precise planning based on forecasts of service demand an exercise in futility until project implementation is under way.

It is now clear to observers, energy developers, and community leaders that the uncertainty created by energy development is both dramatic and sobering. Everyone is now aware of the paradox of large-scale energy development: adequate service provision requires major, up-front (and continuing) planning and financial investment. Yet the pattern of resource development is so uncertain that these investments are highly risky–reality may not correspond to forecasts–and have a disconcerting potential for leaving local communities, and decision-makers, holding the bag.

Many of the community-and state-level decision-makers involved in providing facilities and services to energy resource communities during the 1970s feel they were misled rather than helped by the detailed forecasts used in the planning and permitting process, by the assurance that growth would continue, and by the emphasis on service standards and needs rather than on response strategy. The dramatic turnaround from growth to decline in the 1980s heightened recognition of the uncertainties which surround corporate and/or federal plans for resource development and of the vulnerability of local service providers and decision-makers who stand to lose both from overly aggressive as well as overly conservative response to development forecasts.

Recent legislation has increased the leverage of local decision-makers over energy developers. The experience of the late 1970s and early 1980s, when planned development disappeared at the same time as assurances to the contrary were being given to local leaders, will be remembered and attested to in the permit requirements of the 1980s and 1990s. In those agreements the trade-offs among the various uncertainties will be manifest. Whether communities will adopt a strategy of higher per worker "service charges" to the companies (abandoning elaborate assessments of local service demand as a basis for calculation) or one utilizing an elaborate monitoring and compensation adjustment program remains to be seen.

Similar problems of uncertainty face provincial and federal government officials in the sparsely populated energy resource areas of Canada and Norway, and corporate officials undertaking the development of "new towns" in resource areas where no adequate service and administrative centers exist. The analytic framework developed in this paper could fruitfully be applied to these situations to better understand the mechanisms affecting community service provision in energy resource communities within a variety of organizational contexts.

Notes

1. Indeed, much of the impetus for the inclusion of "socioeconomics" in environmental assessments comes from the realization that the burdens that large-scale projects place on community facilities and services are often excessive, causing adverse social and economic consequences for community residents, and that such impacts, therefore, need to be assessed.

2. The state of Wyoming has sought to reduce this uncertainty through legislation that assures financial assistance to county and municipal jurisdictions undergoing energy development impact. The approximate level of such resources can be forecast in advance using the statutory provisions. However, even in Wyoming, the negotiation process between the energy developer and the affected local jurisdictions importantly influences the resources ultimately allocated to meet growth-induced problems.

3. The funds so derived are often used as the basis for state-local "impact" aid. Such assistance may be provided to local governments on a formula, pass-through basis (aswith oil and gas severancê taxes in Wyoming) or through grants from state agencies established to administer a portion of the severance tax receipts (Montana and North Dakota).

4. An important point about state assistance is that responsibility for service provision remains with the local jurisdiction, with assistance provided in the form of grants to the local government upon request and demonstration of both impact and need. The states have generally not assumed responsibility for ensuring that services needs are met.

5. In all of the discussion of fiscal impacts and uncertainties, it should be noted that, except in the case of jurisdictional mismatches (funds go to one jurisdiction and the impact is experienced in another), large-scale energy developments generally pay for themselves over time. This has provided the opportunity for substantial revenue surpluses in some communities. Better financial management has been recognized as a critical element in minimizing risk and maximizing response capability.

The Delivery and Financing of Housing

D.D. Detomasi

Faculty of Environmental Design
The University of Calgary

I

The social and psychological requirements for a good community are essentially the same everywhere in a given society if not in all societies. However, in the remote and harsh environments of relatively small resource towns, these requirements are both more intense and more difficult to satisfy. The needs of the individual for shelter, privacy and some degree of control over his personal environment are accompanied by a simultaneous need for social interaction and a sense of community. Housing and the residential environment *per se* and in terms of their physical and social linkages with the other elements of the town are critical factors in determining whether the requirements for community can be met in resource towns.

Satisfaction with housing and the residential environment have been related to employee productivity and turnover in resource towns (MacMillan *et al.*, 1974; Healy, 1971; Siemens, 1976) and to a range of social problems (Bradbury, 1980; Brookshire and D'Arge, 1980; Burvill, 1975; Horsfall, 1974). Numerous other studies which have examined some substantive aspect or problem in the development of resource towns conclude that housing and the residential environment are variables which are strongly linked with most other dimensions of community development. Perhaps this is not surprising in view of the role which housing generally plays, at least in North American society.

The problem of providing housing in the appropriate volume, mixture of types, quality and cost, and of creating residential environments which enhance the quality of life in remote resource towns, has long been

41

recognized and has seized the attention of governments, resource development companies and academics.[1] The problems are complex and their
solution requires the resolution of economic and administrative issues
where normal market processes and an appropriate regulatory framework are constrained, distorted or non-existent. Moreover, the nature of
the problem changes through time as one set of issues becomes more or
less important relative to others; for example, economic and environmental factors increasing in importance relative to technological or social
issues.

A number of approaches to providing housing and creating satisfactory residential environments have been devised and implemented
usually with mixed, but predominantly negative, results (see Siemens,
1976). The purpose of this paper is to survey the more important and
common of these approaches and to identify alternatives which might
deserve further exploration and where additional research would be
useful. Two points respecting this survey should be noted here. First, it is
largely confined to the English language literature dealing with the North
American experience, although occasional references to the U.S., the
U.K. or Australia may be used. Second, there is a wealth of empirical
information which is not fully explored in this survey; it is contained in a
number of consultants' reports to industry and government agencies and
in-house studies by governments and corporations, none of which is in
the public domain. This information can be accessed, if at all, only
through an intensive survey of, and interview process with, representatives of these organizations and, as such, is beyond the resources available for this study.[2] In addition to these studies, there is a large number of
case studies of individual resource towns in the U.S. and Canada, many
of which probably discuss housing. A survey of this extensive literature
was also beyond the scope of this study.

II

Housing, like any other asset which yields a stream of services
through time, can be discussed in general and in specific detail in terms
of the traditional economic categories of supply and demand. However,
in the case of resource communities the definition of the critical issues
relevant to housing has tended to focus almost exclusively on supply
problems. To be sure, demand and supply issues are inseparable since
the need to determine what is to be supplied always exists. Nevertheless,
most studies have been concerned with the delivery of a crudely-
estimated volume of housing and the creation of satisfactory residential
environments, with only modest attention given to the various qualitative
dimensions of need or demand. This emphasis on supply and delivery
mechanisms and the neglect of demand issues is a weakness in common
approaches to the problem of housing in boom towns and identifies an
important area for further research.

There are three major phases involved in the provision of housing in a resource community given the anticipated requirements (however determined). First, general land use planning and community and subdivision design activity, assembly and the development of serviced construction sites. Second, the design phase, which involves increasingly detailed decisions respecting residential environment design and housing unit design. During this phase critical decisions respecting unit type, mix, and various qualitative dimensions of housing are made and the possibilities of significant innovations in either the type and form of housing or in the technology of its construction are considered. Third, the construction or delivery phase, during which the housing units, in the quantity, mixture of types and qualities previously determined, are built.

Initially, in the case of new towns, there are two major actors that may be involved in the process; namely, government - usually regional or provincial/state - and the private sector resource developer. In the case of development based on an existing community, two additional, but typically junior, actors will be involved; namely, the existing population as reflected in local government, and the local private economy, particularly the development and construction sector.

Given this set of actors, there are essentially three approaches to the provision of housing in resource communities. Actually, these approaches apply more generally to all aspects of community development - commercial, health, other social services etc. - as well as housing. These methods have been categorized as Public Development, Private Development and Mixed Development respectively.[3] However, it must be noted that both government and the resource developer are typically involved in all three approaches. For example, even in the private method of development (the company town), government is involved in a planning and regulatory role and in the provision of health and/or education services. Similarly, in the public approach to development, the resource company is invol-ved in certain cost-sharing programs for services and facilities. All three approaches have been employed in North America and Western Europe.[4]

In the private method of development, the resource company is responsible for all of the activities in the three phases of housing provision described above. Land acquisition through the private market or, if the community is to be sited on public lands, negotiation with the appropriate government agency, land use planning and allocation, the provision of physical services and infrastructure, the determination of the mixture of housing types and quality, design and construction of housing units are the responsibility of the company.[5] The major role of government is to regulate and control the development process and to ensure the provision of certain public services.

In the public method of development government(s) are responsible for acquisition of non-government lands, for land use planning and land allocation, for the provision of physical services and infrastructure and for the design and construction of housing for government and service sector employees. The design and construction of housing for the employees of a private resource company typically remain the responsibility of the company; indeed, even with public development, the company uses its housing policy as part of its compensation package in an attempt to attract and reduce turnover among employees (Rabnett and Skaburskis, 1977, p. 75).

There are a number of different ways in which responsibilities can be divided under the mixed method of development. The public sector typically retains ownership or control over land and is responsible for land use planning and land allocation decisions. The provision of physical infrastructure and certain social services may be shared, either financially or with each party assuming responsibility for a specific set of activities. Again, the resource company is normally responsible for the design and construction of housing for its employees while government may assume either full or shared responsibility for housing service sector employees.

III

A number of problems have been identified which are related to the various processes that have been used to provide housing in resource communities and to the results in terms of the form and quality of the housing actually provided. The major and most common problems, some of which are clearly interrelated, can be briefly summarized as follows.[6]

   i) the cost of housing and the concept of affordability;
   ii) the existence of a segmented housing market;
   iii) short-term shortages and supply lags in service sector housing markets, both ownership and rental;
   iv) inappropriate unit and residential environment (community) design;
   v) lack of choice, particularly in ownership units;
   vi) lack of choice in tenure options available to service sector employees.

It should be noted that some of these problems reflect an insufficient understanding of the demand side of the housing market, an issue we shall discuss more fully below.

The cost of producing housing in resource towns, both the absolute cost and cost relative to the incomes of the potential consumers, has been a long-standing problem. The reasons for this are largely obvious and well understood and need not be explored in detail here. (However, see A. Robinson, 1976; Choukroun and Jacob, 1976). Costs of land development and construction will typically be high due to the local unavailability of most construction and building materials, shortages of skilled labour, including construction management skills, etc. In the case of new towns, there is no existing land development and building industry and no local suppliers. Regardless of the method of development, almost everything must be imported at significant expense. Even if land is free or relatively cheap, development and construction costs will be high and these can be increased significantly if there are climatic or topographic problems to contend with (Parkinson and Detomasi, 1980). More recently, the relative inflation in land development and construction costs in general and the impact of the high level of prevailing interest rates on large "front-end" expenditures have exacerbated this problem.

In spite of the high wages paid, particularly to employees of the resource company, the cost of housing is still high relative to income earned; thus an affordability problem exists. Resource companies which assume responsibility for housing their employees have devised approaches to the affordability problem which involve subsidy to the employee. The basic approach is to sell (or rent) at market with different forms of subsidy. For example, low interest or interest free loans, which may be fully or partially forgivable after a certain period of time, have been employed. Suncor Corporation in Alberta has employed a 96-month lease to purchase plan. Alternatively, companies can sell housing at prices below market or even below costs. Subsidized ownership units are typically sold with firm buy back provisions whereby an owner who wishes to sell before a specified period has elapsed is required to sell or offer right of refusal to the company. There are variations from company to company in that some offer subsidies only for ownership while others subsidize both ownership and rental. Some offer subsidies only to families/households while others will subsidize singles as well. No matter which approach to subsidy is taken, if it is confined to the employees of the resource company, it will lead to the creation of a segmented housing market in the community. A serious affordability problem will still exist for service sector employees; as Rabnett (1978) has pointed out: "Resource settlements tend to be segmented. There is an adequate supply of subsidized company housing for company households; there is an inadequate supply of unsubsidized housing for service households...This situation is destructive of housing markets". It is also destructive of overall resident satisfaction and a negative factor in the community development of resource towns.

Another approach which has been suggested, but which does not appear to have been attempted, is to raise wage levels for resource company employees so that incomes bear a reasonable relationship to housing costs and housing can be purchased at market prices.[7] Given high construction costs and, more importantly, the high price of housing in markets driven by speculative demand, the required increase in wage levels would be enormous. They would introduce profound distortions into local, regional and, perhaps, national labour markets. At the same time, it will seriously exacerbate the housing affordability problem faced by service sector employees.

Another approach to the cost of housing is to reduce costs through design decisions, innovations and changes in construction techniques and materials. Higher density development, standard size and type units, prefabricated housing, including the use of mobile homes, and modified servicing and construction standards are examples. It is clear that most efforts at achieving cost reduction contributed to the problems of uniformity, lack of choice and poor quality in housing and the larger residential environment noted frequently by commentators on resource town development. These problems and the generally poor quality of urban design are a source of dissatisfaction to many residents in resource towns (Porteous, 1976; Roberts pers. communication). However, it is unclear whether they arise through attempts to reduce cost or simply because of poor design. The latter typically flow from a poor understanding of the special problems of new town design, a misapplication of solutions developed in urban environments, an inadequate knowledge of the demand side of the housing market or simply a lack of concern for environmental quality. Both sets of forces–cost cutting and poor design decisions–are probably contributory.

Even if some cost reductions could be achieved without sacrificing environmental quality and resident satisfaction, the problem of a segmented housing market remains. The employees of the local service sector must meet their housing needs in a market which is typically characterized by inadequate supply, poor quality, restricted choice and a sluggish response to demand pressures. The results are predictable: high rents and house prices, overcrowding, occupation of substandard dwellings. This makes it difficult for government departments and private sector employers to attract and retain employees unless compensating actions are taken. However, compensating measures are also differential. The subsidies required to enable employees to compete in the uncontrolled market may be very large (in Fort McMurray, for example, according to officials of Alberta Housing and Public Works, rent subsidies of 40 to 50 percent were required to secure housing for government workers) and not all employers can afford to pay them. A provincial/state agency can, but a local government or school board cannot; similar differences exist in the private sector. This is a complex problem, one which is usually beyond the ability of local government, employers and the resource company to solve; senior government involvement is necessary.[8]

In spite of excess demand, high rents and prices, and overcrowding, supply of both rental and ownership housing for service sector employees is sluggish and responds only after significant delays, if at all; that is, supply is seldom produced in advance of or even concurrent with demand. In some cases, it responds only modestly even after demand is well-established. This is largely because of the high level of perceived risks inherent in the development of resource based towns. The problems of boom and bust experienced by many resource towns, population turnover, the uncertainties of a finite resource base and similar factors, confront the private developer and builder and financial institutions with the risk that an apparently healthy and growing market can suddenly disappear. The risk sensitivity of private developers, builders and lenders respecting resource towns is well justified by recent events in Canada; the Cold Lake and Alsands Oil sands megaprojects in Alberta, which have recently been stopped, and the shutdown of operations in Uranium City, Saskatchewan, are but two examples where boom turned unexpectedly into bust with unfortunate consequences to the housing industry and to residents who had purchased relatively high-cost housing.

These risks are amplified by the high interest rates and carrying costs associated with land development and building. The threat of unsold building lots and homes and of high vacancy rates in multi-family rental accommodation discourages rapid entry into the construction sector in resource towns and largely explains the sluggishness of housing supply for service sector workers. It probably also helps to explain the extensive and apparently increasing use of mobile homes. Mobile home parks do not typically enhance the quality of the urban environment nor do they offer much variety of choice to residents. However, they can be created relatively quickly and cheaply and, if they threaten to be permanently unoccupied, they can easily be geographically relocated.

It seems clear that if governments are concerned about the quality of the residential environment and the supply of sufficient amounts of quality housing, both rental and ownership, which offers some choice to residents, they must provide it directly or develop programs which limit risk to the private sector. The latter programs would typically involve some sort of guarantee of sales or rentals to private builders and mortgage insurance. Alternatively, governments could require the resource developer to provide housing to service sector employees as part of the resource development approval process. In this case, the resulting community would take on most of the characteristics of the company town, including certain negative features which are inimical to community development. Further, for many potential resource developments, the cost of this policy to the resource company would be prohibitive.

In addition to the considerations respecting the supply side of the housing market briefly discussed above, there are a number of problems, concerns and opportunities on the demand side. In order to make good,or better, choices in various supply side decisions and to develop more effective public policy respecting the provision of housing in resource communities, it is necessary to have a better understanding of some of the demand variables. The next section of this paper addresses this issue.

IV

High rates of labour turnover and a constantly changing population are perhaps the major problems which exist in resource towns and which mitigate community development: Whatever the particular demographic, socioeconomic or ethnic character of the population, few people remain permanently settled in resource towns, despite the high incomes and the provision of facilities intended to meet most social requirements of an urban way of living. After a few years, many families move in search of better employment opportunities, higher level educational facilities or improvement in living standards. (McCann, 1978)

Matthiasson (1971) has documented the relative youth and mobility of workers in resource towns in Canada; for example, a majority of workers interviewed in Fort McMurray were under thirty, had worked in five different communities and expected to be in Fort McMurray for less than five years. With population turnovers of this magnitude, it will require ten to twenty years for a town to acquire the critical mass of permanent population required for a successful community. If the resource upon which the town is based is finite and alternative economic activity is not developed, the resource may be exhausted before community can evolve.

Although empirical evidence is scarce and somewhat mixed (see, e.g., Cumming and Mehr, 1977), recent studies indicate that housing and the residential environment are important determinants of resident satisfaction in resource towns and which influence decisions to remain in a community (Roberts, pers. communication). However, in spite of both theoretical arguments and empirical evidence, many resource towns continue to be built as dull, unimaginative, inferior replicas of urban subdivisions, which offer inappropriate mixtures of type and design features incongruent with the needs and expectations of the population. It was suggested above that one reason for this is the attempt to economize–to reduce the cost of housing in remote locations. Another is "...the well-founded lack of confidence, on the part of corporations and workers alike, in the long-term life of the community" (Stelter and Artibise, 1978). However, a major contributing factor is that we do not know enough about the characteristics of the demand for housing in resource towns in order to make planning and design decisions with confidence. This is particularly the case if innovations in form, construction etc. are being considered.

In a typical urban housing market, there is sufficient variety to permit residents to exercise choice and optimise with respect to their own particular tastes, preferences and income levels. They can choose between owning and renting, between single family and multiple-family forms. They can trade off size, location, aural and visual privacy, environmental amenity and design details against one another in order to satisfy their own particular requirements. This is not the case, of course, in most resource towns where there is no real housing market and no existing housing stock from which to choose. Planning and design decisions and construction must occur before demand characteristics are known; there is only one chance and errors are difficult and costly to rectify. The housing provided will be occupied, there are no alternatives; but if it is inconsistent with the needs and preferences of the residents, they will not be happy and they are not likely to stay.

We have developed some relatively sophisticated models for housing in resource boom towns (Rink and Ford, 1978). Population forecasting models, driven by fairly accurate data respecting the resource company work force and, through multiplier analysis, induced service sector employment, yield estimates from which forecasts of the number of housing units required can be made. Demographic data–age, sex, family size, etc.–which is of variable quality from case to case, permits estimates of the numbers of various types of units required. Payroll and income data and construction cost data give some indication of the split between single versus multiple housing forms and the ownership-rental mix which the market can sustain. This is about as far as we have gone and even here errors in demographic analysis, income and cost estimates and in assumptions respecting tastes, preferences and income allocation decisions, can lead to inappropriate planning and design decisions.

We need to know more about the qualitative and behavioural aspects of the demand for housing in resource towns. For example, we need more (better, some?) information respecting such questions as (the list is only illustrative and not in any order of priority):

Given income levels, is ownership preferred to rental and upon what factors does this depend?

For those who prefer and can afford single family housing:

–Given cost, what is the trade-off between house size and lot size?

–What is the trade off between lot size and location?

–What are critical unit design features and what will be traded off (e.g., income, size, other design features) to obtain them?

For multiple family housing, what are critical design features and what will be traded off (e.g., income, size, other design features) to obtain them?

For various types of housing and tenure, what are the trade offs among preferences respecting the individual housing unit, the larger residential environment and urban form variables?

The tools to examine these questions clearly exist. Social research techniques provide the methodological framework needed to generate much of the information required for an analysis of many aspects of housing demand. Further, the approach of trade-off games, which has been used extensively in studies of urban and suburban housing preferences (Robinson et al. 1975) can be used to elicit the preferences and explore the trade-off issues raised in the preceding questions. Indeed, trade-off games have been used in a recent study of five resource communities in Canada (Robinson, Roberts, pers. communication).

The major problem, of course, in implementing demand and preference studies and applying trade-off games, prior to or as part of the planning and design phases of housing production in resource towns, is that the population to be investigated is not identified. Except in those cases where an employer intends to transfer an existing operations workforce or where the employer is hiring well in advance of the commencement of operations, it is not possible to identify the new residents. In either of the prior cases it would be possible, not only to investigate the nature of the demand for housing in that population but also to involve them directly in the planning and design of their housing and, perhaps, in construction and delivery as well. We shall return briefly to the latter possibility below. In any event, it is not likely that the population of service sector employees will be known and the problem of understanding their housing requirement remains.

The fact is that usually we will not be able to identify the new residents of a resource town ex ante. However, this does not necessarily imply that we know or can learn nothing about certain elements of their demand for housing. It may be possible to use the residents of existing resource towns as surrogates for the unknown populations. There is a substantial case study literature on resource communities in North America (e.g., Gartrell, 1979; Matthiasson, 1970; Porteous, 1974, 1976; Riffel, 1975; Summers et al., 1976). A survey of this literature was beyond the scope of this study, since few dealt specifically with housing or with explicit attempts to obtain information respecting housing demand. However, the studies surveyed did indicate that residents of resource towns do share some general attitudes and characteristics (including a fairly consistent preference for single family detached housing forms). It may be that a more exhaustive survey of the existing literature will reveal that residents of resource towns share a large number of characteristics and attitudes. Unfortunately, the author has been unable to identify a published survey of this extensive case study literature.

The point is that if residents of different resource communities share a number of general characteristics and attitudes, as seems to be the case, then it is likely that they will also share more specific characteristics and attitudes with respect to housing and the residential environment. If this is also the case, and recent research on a small number of communities indicates that it is (Robinson, Roberts, pers. communications), then further studies of resident preferences and trade-off decisions in existing communities should provide information relevant to more sensitive design decisions and to other improvements in the quality of the larger residential environment.

It is obvious that the preceding argument is not uniquely relevant to housing; it is equally applicable to the provision of other goods and services, both public and private. Indeed, the impression one obtains from the literature is that the information provided by studies of existing resource towns and their residents has been used in planning for the provision of services in new resource communities. This seems to be particularly true for social services such as health care, education, recreation and welfare. However, there is not much evidence that such studies have played a major role in planning and design decisions for housing in these communities. It may be that the case study literature does not provide information which would be useful to housing planners and designers; it may also be that they have not been aware or made use of relevant information which does exist to a sufficient extent. In any case, it seems likely that carefully designed studies of existing towns could provide information which could improve housing decisions respecting new communities. However, it may also be that this housing will be more expensive to produce, thus exacerbating the affordability problem.

One approach to the design and construction of housing which is being adapted more frequently in urban centres, but which does not appear to have been employed in resource communities in North America, involves various forms of self-help, including housing cooperatives. An attractive feature of this approach is that it automatically incorporates knowledge of a number of the qualitative dimensions of the demand for housing into the supply decisions for housing. It does this by involving the consumer/resident in the supply process, sometimes as early as the community planning and design stage, sometimes only at the detailed unit design and construction stage.

All self-help approaches to housing have the objectives of reducing the cost of the housing unit while simultaneously providing design features which are more congruent with the preferences of the resident. The cooperative housing approach, in many cases, embodies additional social or political objectives such as community involvement and participation in design, construction and management activities.

A common self-help approach involves the notion of "sweat equity" in a formal way. Once basic land use planning, community design and basic unit design decisions have been made, the resident is given the opportunity to purchase an unfinished dwelling unit. Because of its unfinished state, the cost is substantially below the market price of a finished unit. The resident is then free, within the constraints of usual codes and regulations, to finish the unit as he chooses. In some cases, many internal walls or partitions are missing. Thus, the resident is able to arrange internal spaces and to choose finishing materials, appliances, etc. in such a way as to achieve his preferred trade-off mix, given his income constraint. There are, of course, some institutional and financial constraints which limit the extent to which this approach can be taken. Building codes, fire regulations and the like, and reservations respecting the competence of the owner-builder, require that the unit be completed to a specific minimum extent before it can be turned over and impose other constraints on the choices which can be made in finishing the unit. Similarly, traditional mortgage-lending institutions are reluctant to lend money for the purchase of unfinished units; they may prove difficult to resell in the event of default. In the case of a new resource town this problem should not be as serious. Given the financial involvement of both resource development companies and governments in the provision of housing, it should not be difficult for either or both working together to finance self-help housing of this type.

Cooperative housing is another approach to self-help which holds promise for improving the quality and acceptability of housing in resource towns. The author has been unable to find evidence that this approach has been attempted in new resource communities, although it may be the case that co-ops have been employed in some expanding communities. However, this approach was being seriously investigated by at least one major energy resource development company prior to the cancellation/postponement of the oil sands megaprojects in Alberta (P. Trehearne, D. Stewart pers. comm.).

A housing cooperative has both economic and social objectives. By delivering housing at cost, a unit of given type and quality can be provided at a price substantially below market. By achieving economies of scale in the use of construction labour and through bulk purchasing of building materials and supplies, a co-op is able to produce a unit at lower cost than an individual owner-builder could achieve. In addition, the "sweat equity" option in finishing and detailing can be used in a cooperative program to reduce costs further.

Cooperative housing can embrace both ownership and rental forms of tenure and it offers the opportunity to involve the eventual tenants at the earliest stages of the housing planning and design process. Thus, many of the critical characteristics of the demand for housing, which are generally not known to suppliers, are known from the beginning. In addition, the organization of housing cooperatives creates an excellent vehicle for the development of both social organization and sense of community among a population who are otherwise newcomers and strangers. Public participation in the planning and urban development processes has been advocated for more than twenty years (Warren, 1966). A cooperative, even if its primary focus is housing, would provide an organizational framework for such participation by citizens.

Cooperative housing has been eligible for senior government financial assistance in Canada since 1944 (Lips, 1977). However, public policy in support of cooperative housing efforts was largely lacking until 1973. Up until that time, cooperatives were considered and funded on an *ad hoc* basis; no general program for funding or otherwise assisting in the development of housing cooperatives existed till then. In 1973, a number of amendments to the National Housing Act resulted in a Cooperative Housing Program and since that date both federal and provincial governments have developed a number of initiatives to facilitate and provide financial assistance for this type of housing (Kloppenburg, 1982).

Almost all, if not all, of the cooperative housing projects in Canada have been built in the larger urban centres; this is where the need and demand for this form of housing is the most serious and where the critical mass of population needed to organize and manage a co-op exists. However, although there are some obvious difficulties in resource towns which are not relevant to cities, there is no reason in principle why co-op housing could not be attempted there.

The major problem, of course, is that co-ops are largely social organizations which are created and maintained by people with common objectives and who share certain values. In the case of a resource town where the population to be housed are strangers prior to their coming to the town, there is no mechanism by which this social organization can arise prior to their arrival, at which time they must be housed. It is hard to imagine that even serious attempts by the resource developer and/or government agencies to assist in the creation of a housing co-op could accomplish much prior to the arrival of the new population. The exception to this would be the case where the employees of the resource developer were a workforce which was simply being transferred en masse from one location to another.

Once the population is in the new town, at least the possibility of a housing cooperative being formed exists. If the new residents are or perceive themselves to be *permanently* housed (however well) then the underlying need for an alternative housing form and process is largely eliminated. It may be that the only way to facilitate the development of a cooperative, or any delivery process which requires knowledge of the qualitative characteristics of housing demand, is to ensure that the housing initially available to new residents is perceived as being *temporary*, the mobile home is an obvious possibility.

The author cannot judge whether the advantages of offering residents an opportunity to participate in the planning, design and construction of permanent housing - housing which would obviously more closely meet their needs, preferences and expectations - after their arrival in the community would offset the disadvantages to the resource developer and other employers of not having a completed instant town with which to attract new employees. However, it would seem that the resources which both resource developers and governments are willing to devote to the provision of housing in resource towns would be more than adequate to finance alternative forms of housing delivery. Given the important role which housing plays in worker satisfaction and performance and in resident satisfaction with the community, an experiment with the more demand-sensitive approaches outlined above might be well worthwhile.

Notes

1. A number of useful and extensive bibliographies, covering the general topics of boom towns, resource towns and company towns, as well as the specific areas of housing and residential development, have been compiled; a number of the entries date from the late nineteenth century. (See Gunder, 1980; Levenson, 1977; Maguire, 1980; and Pressman, 1982.)

2. The author is aware that such a study "Housing Strategies forResource Town Development" has just been completed for the Canada Mortgage and Housing Corporation by Professor L. Pinfield of Simon Fraser University. The study extended over a period of two years and received funding in excess of $18,000. The final report, which has recently been submitted to CMHC should be available in the Fall, 1982. Professor Pinfield, although reluctant to discuss the results of his work prior to the submission of his final report, has kindly provided the author with useful bibliographical assistance.

3. An excellent survey of these three methods of development, including a description of the management and organizational framework required for each, and a description and assessment of the major benefits and costs associated with each can be found in Rabnett and Skaburskis (1977).

4. For example, and extensive bibliography on company towns Levenson, 1977) identifies privately developed communities based on textiles, all of the major mineral industries, smelting, food processing and manufacturing in the U.S., Canada, the U.K., Scandinavia, Germany and Italy. Publicly developed communities in the U.S. and Canada have been based on hydro electric and atomic energy, national parks, and other government services as well as natural resource development.

5. In some jurisdictions, government may become involved in the design and construction of housing for government and other service sector employees. In these situations, differences between "markets" for company provided housing and that provided by the public sector can be a source of problems, particularly for the latter. This issue is discussed further below.

6. For a useful discussion of some of these problems and alternative policy approaches to them, see Rabnett et al., 1978, from which the above survey draws. Also see Bradbury, 1980; Siemens, 1976; I.B.I., Pressman, 1976.

7. This approach was apparently considered by Esso Resources in its planning for the heavy oil megaproject at Cold Lake, Alberta; it is not clear whether this issue had been resolved at the time the project was shelved in 1981. One wonders what the response of local private service sector employers and government agencies would have been if wages paid to the resource employees had risen sufficiently to close the affordability gap.

8. The two solutions, namely, the forced creation of an undifferentiated housing market or subsidies, equivalent to those provided by the resource developer to its employees, to all service sector employees, both require vigorous senior government interaction. For a further discussion, see Rabnett et al., 1978. pp. 25-30.

Changes in Economic Structure and Employment Alternatives Arising from a Major Economic Development Event

Ron Shaffer

Department of Agricultural Economics,
University of Wisconsin,
Madison, Wisconsin

Eirik Vatne

Institute of Industrial Economics,
Bergen, Norway

Since the early 1970's, sophistication in projecting the social-economic changes that occur in small communities as a result of a major economic development event has increased greatly. The body of literature discussing *anticipated changes* is fairly extensive. However, the literature on *actual changes* is less coordinated and less comprehensive partially because it is largely found as working papers or as contract reports.

From the perspective of the social science profession, a major limitation of *ex post* analysis is the great difficulty in distinguishing development impacts from ongoing trends. Regardless of these limitations, there remains a need to synthesize the literature reporting actual changes in communities in order to identify gaps in our understanding. In the balance of this paper we will synthesize the literature regarding the actual changes in the economic structure and the actual changes in employment opportunities in the community as a result of an economic development event. We will examine only smaller communities that were originally agricultural in nature, or relied heavily upon a single nonfarm industry, where a minimum of 1,000 new jobs were created or there was at least a 50% change in the community's employment base.

A general summary of the empirical literature from the U.S., Canada, Scandinavia, and Scotland indicates that the studies are of specific

55

events, focus upon points in time for their measurements rather than analysis of trends and do not disaggregate results for specific segments of the population or economy. The end result is that it is very difficult to link specific types of community change with types of events, or characteristics of the host community. We have a good understanding of the general changes that occur following a major economic development event, but we are only beginning to ask questions about how and why these changes occur and which segments of the population and community are affected.

CHANGES IN ECONOMIC STRUCTURE

Our concern is with secondary changes, particularly the ownership/control of secondary investment, the location of the secondary changes and the timing of the secondary changes. Linked and consumer businesses are two types of secondary changes that may occur in a community's economic structure because of an economic development event. Linked businesses are those either supplying inputs or providing further processing of the output from the primary business. Consumer business is supply of goods and services to local and area households and families.

Linked Businesses

The economic development event affects linked businesses in two ways: through purchases from existing businesses, and through the appearance of new firms. The evidence about which occurs is mixed for both energy and nonenergy development events.

Shaffer, Fischer and Pulver (1982, p. 128) indicated that the proportion of local supplies purchased declined as the size of manufacturing plants (that located) increased, and the linkage in the local economy varied between material and service inputs. They concluded that the concept of linkages needed to be broadened to include the traditional linkages between independently owned businesses and internal linkages among divisions within a large corporate structure. In twelve energy resource communities, Gilmore et al. (1981, p. 80) found little local purchasing. What there was appeared to be limited to expendable supplies. Local merchants could not meet the input requirements (quality, quantity and timeliness) of the energy firm.

Funk (1964, pp. 85-89) asked Clinton Engines for information about purchases from local firms. In the first year of operation (1951), the plant purchased $158,572 from four firms. This had increased to purchases of $369,498 from 12 firms by 1961. However, one firm accounted for one-third of the local purchases. His analysis did not indicate if any of these linked businesses were new to the community. Werner's survey (1980, p.

26) of oil and gas development in Montana yielded evidence that local firms had expanded, new firms had started and new branches of outside firms had located in the area. A comparison of telephone directory listings indicated between 1978 and 1980 oil related business listings increased from 82 to 125. Using *County Business Patterns* data, Werner found 300 businesses in the impacted county in 1977. Over the next 29 months, 382 additional business establishments appeared. The type of business (linked/consumer) or the type of growth (new/expansion) was not reported.

Berg (1965) found that an aluminum smelter's local purchases accounted for only 5.3% of total sales in the Ardal kommune in Norway. Vatne (1979) estimated that an ammonia fertilizer plant near Telemark, Norway purchased only 1% of its inputs locally and 23% from within the county. Two Norwegian studies of the Mongstad refinery demonstrated that the local purchases increased from 1.5% in the construction phase to 5.5% a year later (1975) in the production phase (Eskedal, 1974; Kirkenes and Enoksen, 1976). An additional 6.8% was purchased in the region (Bergen) during construction; this rose to 9% in the production phase.[1]

Proportion of Inputs Purchased Locally

	Folgefann	Grytten
TOTAL	5.3%	23.5%
Goods	2.2	11.3
Services	12.2	54.4
Transportation/digging	14.2	59.3
General Construction Material	6.5	65.0
General Building Material	4.4	17.3

Gilmore, Moore and Hammond's analysis (1976) suggests that linked support businesses appeared only after a sufficient agglomeration had occurred (a long-run phenomenon). The Shaffer, Fisher and Pulver survey (1982, p. 129) revealed that suppliers often avoided tight local labor markets that were dominated by a single large firm and so further reduced the emergence of linked businesses. When Gilmore *et al.* (1981, p. 80) extended their analysis to look at linked industries that had appeared in the communities as a result of the energy development projects, there were none identified in nine communities, and two communities had no hard evidence either way. Leistritz and Maki (1981, p. 44) found a minimal amount of energy linked support businesses appearing in McLean County as a result of the Coal Creek mine and electric generating project.

The evidence of the effect on linked businesses is mixed. The impact occurs both as increased sales to existing firms and the appearance of new firms. Yet major purchases of supplies and services locally appears to be unlikely in smaller communities.

Consumer Businesses

In general consumer impact will be related to where and how the workers spend their additional income. This will be determined largely by the amount of goods and services offered within the local community vis á vis nearby competing communities. Are the new consumer goods/services provided by expansion of existing business, or do new businesses appear? Are the new businesses in competition with existing businesses?

The change in consumer sales will vary among communities and product lines. One study of Iowa farm families working at a new plant found that 50% of the families increased their shopping in the community where the plant had located. Of those who had increased their shopping, 74% reduced the amount of shopping they had previously done in other communities (Kaldor et al. 1964). Funk's analysis (1964, pp. 90-91) of the Clinton Engine Co. impacts among eastern Iowa communities indicated that 85% of the food and household product firms and personal goods and services firms indicated that they experienced an increase in their sales, 80% of the professional services indicated a sales increase, and 91% of the automotive businesses indicated a positive effect on their local sales. Furthermore, when comparing Census of Business data between 1948 and 1959, he found that retail and service trade increased by 61.5% in the impacted county and only 32.3% in the control counties (Funk 1964, p. 95). This was similar to the changes estimated by comparing sales tax receipts for the same area. Leistritz and Maki (1981, pp. 88,90) reported that total sales tax receipts increased by 38.72% in the impacted county and by 22.39% in the primary and secondary impacted areas between 1974 and 1976.

Beyond the change in the volume of sales in the trade-service sector is the appearance of new consumer businesses. Davis (1963, p.213) partially itemized the new businesses that were established in Searcy, Arkansas in the 1950-59 decade following a manufacturing plant location: 23 grocery, 3 furniture and hardware, 3 automotive supply, 12 department and dry goods, 1 drug and 22 others. Leistritz and Maki (1981, p. 88) reported that the number of trade and service establishments in McLean County increased from 186 to 215 and 67 to 146 respectively between 1972 and 1977. Coon et al.'s study (1976, p. 23) of the ABM project found that during the construction period, the number of retail and service firms in one impacted county increased 15.3% and 13.3%

respectively. Prior to the construction period, retail, service and wholesale firms had been experiencing a decline. Another impacted county had 27 new businesses formed, 18 were expanded, rebuilt or relocated, and 18 changed hands. The project definitely reversed a trend of decline in local business activity but, again, the causes behind which type of change occurred are not clear.

Control of Secondary Businesses

Do local entrepreneurs anticipate the changes that are going to occur and assemble the capital to meet those needs, or is it outside capital and developers who own the new businesses or buy out local businesses? Local entrepreneurs may combine with nonlocal entrepreneurs to provide the secondary business development (partnerships and franchises). Furthermore, if the municipality has implemented some form of downtown redevelopment, or land assembly, etc., there can be a significant public/private partnership.

A commercial establishment operating in the pre-development phase of a community is typically described as operating with a minimal profit margin, little incentive or history of capital investments, a diversified inventory appealing to a wide range of customers and a passive marketing program. These characteristics are not necessarily good precursors for that business to anticipate and accommodate the substantial changes of the development phase. "Not everyone is up to the challenge" (Cortese and Jones, 1977, p. 80).

Murdock and Leistritz (1979, p. 167) suggest that there was insufficient data to confirm or deny the prevalent concern about the ability of local business to compete with or be replaced by the national chain or affiliate. Gray (1969, p. 29) found that when a Kaiser aluminum plant located in West Virginia, most of the local people did not have the capital or the entrepreneurial experience to start new businesses. Branch or chain stores were the source of the expansion. Leistritz and Maki (1981, p. 44) found that the new or expanded trade and service facilities in McLean County, North Dakota were operated by either local individuals or people who had been native to the area and had returned because of increased local economic activity. Their interviews with community leaders suggested that the competition from new businesses was not significant. However, much of the consumer purchases in the project were occurring outside the impacted county in nearby trade centers. All that the local merchants were doing was performing a convenience function. A study by Thompson *et al.* (1978) noted that the changes in sales volume went to existing establishments. While this suggests that local entrepreneurs were capturing that additional activity, their evidence does not indicate whether or not stores had changed hands, nor had they tracked the changes over a long period of time. Again, the empirical evidence is mixed and there is no systematic analysis of what factors causes differences in the community response.

A major economic development event and the associated secondary business activities can alter community capital flows and requirements in at least two ways (Thompson 1980, p. 91). First, the development event should increase capital needs of local businesses. The second change in the flow of capital occurs from consumers' needs to purchase durables such as household furnishings, housing, etc. These changes in capital requirements are related to the ownership question through the source of financing for the new secondary economic activity. Can local equity or debt capital sources meet the new capital demands of the secondary business investments? Moriarty (1980, p. 17) suggests that the capital for most of the secondary investment will come from outside the impacted community. The evidence of ownership/control changes is limited. There are no studies of how these changes might be affected by the size of the development event and the speed of the development. Other remaining questions include: How do local capital sources evaluate and judge the feasibility of proposals, given the inherent uncertainty about the major event? What types of mechanisms are used to attract external capital into the community while maintaining local control?

Location of Secondary Investments

Does secondary development occur in a site that opens up new commercial areas, or is it in the existing commercial areas? If it is in an existing commercial area, it is more likely to support existing businesses. Does the secondary development occur within the impacted community or in adjacent communities?

The Gilmore *et al.* survey (1981) of twelve energy projects indicated that while retail sales had increased, they had failed to increase at the rate anticipated because of a substantial amount of nonlocal spending. Nearby areas that had been trade centers prior to development continued to maintain and reinforce that position after the event. For one project, a regional shopping center outside the impacted area captured a significant proportion of the additional activity. Another community experiencing significant local impacts had made a recent downtown revitalization effort. In other communities there was a minimal amount of change attributable to the development event. Leistritz and Maki (1982, p. 12) found that while the impacted communities experienced substantial increases in trade and service activity, the vast majority of the additional consumer spending occurred in the nearby regional trading centers of Bismarck and Mandan. On the other hand, Kaldor and Bauder (1963) found that about half the families with husbands or wives employed at the Clinton Engines Corporation reduced their spending in other communities and increased it in the community where the plant was located. Ten of the 19 communities that lost shopping had less than 1,000 people, five had 1,000-5,000, and four had populations exceeding 30,000. All of these communities were within sixty miles of the plant site. They also found the shift of shopping towards the plant site community was not uniform across all consumer goods and services. Groceries and clothing were more frequently mentioned as part of that shift, while household furnishing, hardware, gasoline, oil and car repairs, doctors and dentists were less frequently involved.

The extent to which the secondary investments occur in the local versus other areas depends on several factors. Gilmore *et al.* (1981, p. 104) concluded:

1. the proportion of the work force that were in-commuters reduced local consumption;

2. existing excess capacity in the trade/service sector absorbed the additional demand;

3. that there was a lag in response by the local commercial sector to increased demands;

4. that there was a local business attitude that the changes are just transitory and one would just suffer through those few months of tight markets and not overinvest; and*

5. that the purchasing policies of the firm itself consciously seeking out local suppliers and encouraging their development could increase local investments.

The latter is unlikely (Shaffer *et al.* 1982, pp. 128-129).

Timing of Secondary Business Investments

Does secondary investment precede the development in anticipation of changes, does it occur concurrently, or does it occur after the development is well underway and the development's characteristics are relatively firmly established? If secondary business investments occur in anticipation of the development, what sources of information do entrepreneurs use to make those decisions? If they occur before the development has started, how do secondary investors keep abreast of changing development patterns and schedules such that their investments are appropriate? Given the uncertainty in scheduling, the magnitude of major projects and moderately risk-adverse investors, much of the secondary private business investment would lag behind the primary investment schedules. The recent experiences of the Colorado Shale

Project and Imperial's Cold Lake tar sands project would reinforce the reluctance on the part of the businesses (local and nonlocal) to make anticipatory investments. Gilmore et al. (1981, pp. xiii, 77) found that retail trade and local service sectors activity appeared following the peak construction period and resulted in excess capacity.

CHANGE IN EMPLOYMENT ALTERNATIVES

The primary employment changes for a given economic development are determined by the size, composition, and timing of the event. The literature is replete with extensive reporting of the size and composition (age, sex, race, skills). To summarize the extensive literature on labor force composition again (Summers et al. 1976; Murdock and Leistritz 1979) is not necessary. The focus of our review will be changes in the local labor market, primary and secondary occupational changes, the timing of changes, and finally the source of labor.

One of the more extensive examinations of secondary employment demand was that by Funk (1964) of the Clinton Engine Co. location in an Eastern Iowa community. He reported that 27.3% of the firms in the impacted community hired additional labor as a result of direct demand from Clinton Engines. These secondary employment increases averaged 0.64 workers per firm. For businesses in the balance of the county, only 3.8% indicated they had hired additional workers, and the average was 0.05 workers per firm. Additional workers hired per firm varied by type of firm. Farm related businesses added, on the average, only 0.33 workers, while there were 2.83 workers added in public services and utility firms and 1.47 workers in the construction industry. For other businesses in the community, anywhere from 0.4 to 0.6 workers were added.

Numerous other studies have found changes in the total employment and specific sectors of an impacted community's economy (Murdock and Leistritz 1979; Summers et al. 1976). While important, the changes in sectoral employment are less useful for manpower analysis which is concerned with the skills required and available.

Occupational Change

While there is a great similarity among energy development events, the primary occupational changes varied with the type of event that occurred and by development phase. The core development firm knows approximately the types of workers it will require, when it will require them and the minimum number that it requires (Gilmore et al. 1981; Stenstavold, 1979). Secondary occupational changes are much less obvious because of variation in investment decisions by various entrepreneurs and the types of investments that occur locally. Measurement of aggregate secondary job changes often fails to identify occupational needs and the timing of demands.

Hannah and Mossier (1977) identified occupations that experienced shortages of people available to fill job openings. The nonenergy related construction industry experienced shortages in carpenters, electricians, plumbers and brick masons. Public agencies experienced shortages of police, maintenance, and clerical workers. The commercial services experienced shortages of retail sales clerks, food service workers, auto repairs, and hotel/motel maids. There was also a shortage of doctors, dentists and lab technicians in the health profession. While this information does not give a direct measure of secondary changes in the occupational structure, it does indicate that the change in demand for these occupations exceeded the ability of the community and area to supply.

A major economic development event would naturally be presumed to alter the occupational structure and mobility of a community, but the evidence is inconclusive. Sommers (1958) found that return migrants to a West Virginia aluminum rolling mill took jobs that had a lower occupational level than their previous jobs. Beck (1972, p. 13) suggests that the rate of change in occupations by residents of a community did not seem to vary as a result of a major industrial development event. However, those individuals interested in changing occupations did have a wider choice of occupations. Murdock and Schriner (1978, pp. 435, 443) divided nine communities in Montana, North Dakota, Utah and Wyoming into pre-development, currently developing (construction) and post-development (a military base closedown). Using the results of 1,424 interviews, they found that 17.8% of the residents in the pre-development, 24.1% in the currently developing and 19% in the post-development communities had experienced upward occupational mobility. Also, rates of downward occupational mobility for both long-time and new residents were considerably greater in the pre-development and post-development communities. Krahn and Gartrell (1981) found that almost half of male in-migrants in a new town experienced a change in occupational status (half up and half down). Thirty-eight percent of the oil industry workers and only 22% of the non-oil industry workers improved their occupational status as a result of their in-migration to Fort McMurray. While migration did allow considerable mobility into core industries (and better jobs) those who were able to find employment with the two large oil companies (Syncrude and Suncor) experienced greater mobility (higher returns to previous status and education).

Murdock and Leistritz (1979, pp. 82-89) found considerable occupational stability since most of the construction workers were holding jobs that were similar to their previous occupations. Their survey of previous employment for coal mine and power plant workers in North Dakota and Wyoming indicated that construction and other mining accounted for 39% of the coal industry employees in North Dakota.

Geographic Spread of Employment Change

Gilmore et al. (1981, pp. 74-76) note that the actual increase in retail-service employment in the impacted communities was less than anticipated. Much of that increase in spending occurred elsewhere. They also found that the presence of an indigenous construction work force yielded community changes that were smaller and less disruptive. The availability of housing, shopping facilities and local services, including schools, were important in influencing where the nonindigneous construction work force was likely to settle. Construction workers often settle in slightly larger, better-serviced communities, even though the communities might be further away from the project site.

Changes over Time

For both primary and secondary employment the skills required change between construction, operation and the development of secondary business investments. Gilmore et al. (1981) found that during the early construction phase most of the workers were laborers, carpenters, and concrete workers, with some operating/engineering categories. In later construction phases the workers tended to be iron workers, pipe-fitters, boiler makers and electricians. Leistritz and Maki (1981, p. 5) found that in the early years iron workers, laborers, and operators were the most frequently used craftsmen, while electricians, pipefitters and boiler makers were the major crafts at the end of the construction period. We found no studies examining the secondary occupational changes over time.

Labor Supply

What type of labor is available to fill the new jobs? What type of training and skills do the residents have and what type of on-the-job training is conducted? What is the labor force participation rate and how many new labor force entrants will be attracted? What proportion of the total job needs will be filled by local workers, in-commuters and in-migrants?

There are essentially five major sources of workers: currently unemployed workers, new entrants to the labor force, workers shifting among local businesses, in-commuters, and in-migrants. Distribution among these sources is heavily dependent upon: (1) the size of the population base; (2) the extent of similar types of economic activity in the area, either previously or concurrently; and (3) the scheduling of the project.

The local unemployed have not been a major source of labor. Summers *et al.* (1976) reported that most direct employment contained less than 10% who had been previously unemployed. One would anticipate that local unemployed would fill some new secondary jobs or refill vacated jobs. Gilmore *et al.* (1981, p. 81) found that the unemployment rate generally declined in the impacted communities, but other forces in the local economy contributed to the decline and there were periods when unemployment actually increased. This general decline would imply that the unemployed are filling some secondary jobs, but a simple increase in the labor force may reduce the unemployment rate without necessarily reducing the number unemployed. There generally is no hard evidence about the proportion of local unemployed workers who find jobs because of the energy development project. An exception is the Krahn and Gartrell paper (1981), which found that 29% of the males in the Fort McMurray labor force were unemployed before they migrated to the town. The proportion was similar for those employed in primary (30%) and secondary firms (29%).

The number of primary jobs filled at energy development projects by new labor force entrants appears highly variable. Murdock and Leistritz (1979, p. 86) report that 18.9% of North Dakota coal employees surveyed in 1974 had no previous employment, while only 0.6% of the Wyoming uranium workers surveyed had been previously unemployed. Some studies reported increased labor force participation rates (Murdock and Leistritz 1979; Summers *et al.* 1976) but do not account for ongoing trends.

Local job shifting can be a major source of labor for new primary and secondary jobs created in the community. Brady's survey (1974, p. 49) of three manufacturing plants employing 1,250 workers indicated that 32.8% of the workers had shifted within the community. Funk's analysis (1964, pp. 150-152) indicated that 24% of the firms in the impacted Iowa community felt that they had lost employees to Clinton Engines in the preceding ten years. Their loss averaged 0.64 workers per firm, or 12.6% of their 1959 work force. The proportion of firms losing workers ranged from a low of 11.8% for professional service firms to a high of 40% for the construction firms. The firms in the balance of the county felt they had lost an average of 0.15 workers or only 4.7% of their 1959 average employment.

Mackay (1977) acknowledged that local employers complained about the loss of labor and sharp increases in wages from the North Sea Oil development in Scotland. However, he contends that an already existing downward trend was only hastened by oil development. Mackay found that construction workers recruited locally for the Flotta Terminal filled laborer, domestic and secretarial positions. Most came from local government and miscellaneous services, and few came from farming or fishing. For five oil platform construction sites in Scotland the work force was drawn from several sectors, but predominantly from those sectors that used workers with the desired skills, e.g., construction, mechanical engineering, metal manufacturing. Thus, the competition in narrow segments of the labor market sometimes increased dramatically. Stenstavold (1979, p. 126) reported that the different activities associated with the North Sea Oil development attracted the most employees from mining, manufacturing, building and construction. Berge and Ovsthus's (1975) study of the Mongstad refinery in Norway also found that the work force was drawn from several sectors and it varied by specific phase of the refinery project. Construction and related sectors, followed by tertiary activities, were major suppliers of laborers.[2]

PREVIOUS EMPLOYMENT

Project Phase	Primary	Manufacturing	Construction	Tertiary	Home	Other
Refining	2.9%	36.1%	10.5%	35.2%	2.9%	12.4%
Construction	2.5	10.3	62.6	8.4	—	16.2
Installation	—	16.3	42.7	16.0	—	25.3
Catering	8.1	8.1	2.7	37.9	25.7	17.5
TOTAL	2.7	19.9	33.9	22.4	3.9	17.2

From a community perspective, job shifting need not be an adverse response to a major economic development event, especially if vacated jobs are refilled with comparable quality workers. For the most part, Funk (1964) reported that the firms who had lost employees to Clinton Engines had replaced those employees. Of the firms in the impact community losing employees, 90.4% claimed they had replaced them, while only 80% of the firms in the rest of the county that had lost employees replaced them. Examining the data in a slightly different fashion, Funk estimated that, for the entire county, 78.9% of those who shifted had their prior jobs refilled. In the impacted community the ratio was 79.1% and for the balance of the county it was 75%. When the firms experiencing a loss of labor were asked about the quality of the replacements, 55% of the firms in the county said that it was the same, 34% said it was better, and only 10% said it was poorer. Mackay (1977, p. 72) reported that, with two major exceptions, local firms experiencing a worker loss due to construction of St. Fergus Terminal generally were able to adapt. Some vertically integrated firms were unable to replace a few key men and construction firms could not find labor.

The distribution of employment benefits will be affected by the ability of residents to transfer their skills to new jobs and/or residents' ability or willingness to participate in training. Again, the evidence is not conclusive. Helgeson and Zink's examination (1973, p. 41) of the Jamestown industrial experience indicated that 56.6% of the workers felt their former skills were transferable to their new job, yet over half (51%) of the new employees were given on-the-job training. However, of the individuals interviewed, 75% currently held unskilled labor positions in the firm, and only 19.4% held a management position.

Little and Lovejoy (1979) asked workers if they would participate in a training program if it would yield a more desirable job. Only 45.9% said yes, if the training site was local and they were paid to do it. The unemployed workers responded with even less willingness (38.5%) to the same conditions! Only 7.7% and 7.4% of the workers and the unemployed said they would participate if the training was not local and not paid.

Moe's (1972) analysis of the Husnes aluminum smelter in Norway found that many local residents, after taking a job at the smelter, moved into service jobs when they became available. In contrast, Selvik and Hernes (1977) found that once local people entered the local construction work force they tended to move on to new construction sites. Furthermore, the locals tended to fill less skilled jobs and were replaced as the job skills increased over time.

Beyond the local labor pool, in-commuters and in-migrants are a major source of labor. Murdock and Leistritz (1979) found a tremendous variation between the construction and operation phases across fourteen energy related construction projects in seven Mountain and Northern Great Plains states. The percent of construction workers hired from within the community varied from a low of 3.3% in one plant to a high of 78.6% in another. The average proportion of local workers in the construction work force was 39.9%. For operating work forces, the average was 61.8% and the range from 0% to 95.7%. The degree of local labor force hiring was a function of the size of the local labor force, status of other construction products in the area, and the union referral system, coupled with the population of the area and the state. One reason for the high proportion of local hire in the operating force was because the plants had pursued internal promotion programs which permitted local residents to move up within the company. Over half (52%) of the coal mine and power plant workers in North Dakota, and 54% in the Glenrock, Wyoming area had held at least three positions within the current company.

The evidence for in-migration and in-commuting in Norway and Scotland is similar to that found in North America. Gjesteland (1973) found that 42% of the workers at the Ardal aluminum smelter came from the kommune and an additional 23% come from the balance of the fylker (county). Berge and Ovsthus' (1975) examination of construction workers at the Mongstad refinery indicated a substantial in-migration over a two year period with the proportion of workers residing in Nordhordland increasing from 33.2% to 56.1%. The proportion of local residents holding jobs was 78.6% in refinery, 49.0% in construction firms, 24.7% in installation firms and 74.3% in catering firms. Moe's (1972) survey of laborers at the Husnes aluminum smelter found that 30% of the work force was local and 21% commuted from the fylker. Two Norwegian surveys (Selvik and Hernes 1977; Mykleibest 1969) identified 18-40% of the construction workforce at two hydro-power projects as being local residents. Gjesteland (1973) found that 64% of the blue collar occupations at the Ardal aluminum smelter came from within the same county.

The geographic size of the labor market from which a project draws its labor force appears to be related to specific skills. The low skill occupations are generally filled by local workers. Jobs requiring moderate skills use a regional or state labor market, while very highly skilled occupations often draw from a nationwide labor market. Murdock and Leistritz (1979, pp. 76-80) report that on the average, 45.9% of the workers came from the state in which the project was located and 15.8% from adjacent states. Again, the variation among specific plants was quite high.

SUMMARY AND CONCLUSIONS

The amount of literature on actual changes that we were able to uncover was limited in the number of projects examined. Generalizing to other situations should only be done with great caution. There definitely remains an unfilled void in our understanding of the actual changes in employment and economic structure. It is highly unlikely that linked businesses will appear immediately. Local businesses are quite likely to experience an increase in sales, but sales to the project will not be a large proportion of the businesses' sales, nor will the business be a major supplier to the project. The secondary effects in these small communities tended to be minimal when compared to the primary impacts. There is often a fairly wide geographical dispersion of impacts. The empirical studies fail to provide much information on the control/ownership of the secondary development and the timing of those secondary investments and employment changes.

Most of these studies provided little insight to the change in occupational structure beyond crude generalizations about more trade and service employment. The rate at which local residents fill new occupations is highly variable, and depends upon the skills within the local labor force, the hiring practices of the plant, and whether or not it is a permanent operating job or a temporary construction job. Occupational changes occur continually and the extent to which outside workers (in-commuters and in-migrants) are brought in appears to be highly dependent upon nearby population centers and such artificial phenomena as union jurisdictional boundaries. In some cases, it appears that in-migrants were return migrants.

The actual changes experienced in the communities are seldom equal to those of the projections. This may be a self-fulfilling prophecy, but it indicates that single point projections are unlikely to be helpful.

Notes

1. A Norwegian study of local input purchases (Syvertsen and Tuder, 1976) at two hydro-power projects also found minimal local purchases and variations with input and site.

2. Proportion of Workers at Mongstad Refinery by Previous Sector of Employment.

The Impact of a Major Economic Development Event On Community Income Distribution

Glen C. Pulver

Professor, Dept. of Agricultural Economics,
University of Wisconsin-Madison, U.S.A.

Arne Selvik

Director, Institute of Industrial Economics,
Bergen, Norway

Ron Shaffer

Professor, Dept. of Agricultural Economics,
University of Wisconsin-Madison, U.S.A.

INTRODUCTION

Major economic development events are often viewed as a means to improve the personal incomes of residents of the affected community. These events might include resource exploitation, defense installations, manufacturing plants, and other activities which rapidly increase a community's economic base. They are frequently beyond the direct control of those most directly impacted. They are often sited in remote rural areas and, thus, overshadow the local economic structure.

Major economic developments are normally accompanied by increases in funds from sources external to the community. Land and construction expenditures introduce new capital flows in the form of wages, supply purchases, property income, etc. The total impact of these capital flows is amplified by multiplier effects and secondary economic activity within the community. Expansion in housing and commercial and public facilities lead to new capital flows, new wages, profit taking and inflationary pressure on limited community resources (Summers *et al.*, 1976; Summers and Selvik, 1982; Murdock and Leistritz, 1979; Shaffer and Fischer, 1981).

Leaders at the national, regional and local levels are concerned about the substantive impacts of the major economic events on communities. They are interested in changes in employment and income, in other issues such as social structure and environmental quality, and also in anticipating and mitigating potential problems.

Although there is widespread research on the subjects of changes in employment and per capita income resulting from new electric generating plants, manufacturing plants and the like, little is known about their distributive effects (Leistritz *et al.*, 1982a; Summers *et al.*, 1976; Rogers *et al.*, 1978). Policy makers at all levels are concerned, for it is precisely information respecting the impact of development on income distribution which is most useful in decision making regarding the financing of public goods and services (Nelson, 1979).

This paper will summarize the empirical literature on the impact of major economic development on community income distribution. It covers a number of studies dealing with capital control, profit taking, wages, other income, property taxes, and living costs with specific emphasis on their distribution within the community. In this paper, a community is defined as the immediate trade area of a development project.

The first part of the paper outlines a general framework for looking at the question of the distributional effect of major economic developments. The second part is a presentation of the results extracted from previous research. Finally, conclusions respecting the adequacy of current knowledge about the distributional effects of development are presented.

FRAMEWORK OF ANALYSIS

The distribution of the shock of any major economic development event will change through time. No two major economic developments will generate the same consequences. An electric generating plant fueling an aluminum smelter in a remote fjord in Norway will produce a different specific economic consequence than oil sands exploitation in Northern Canada, or an industrial plant in the central U.S.A. Each will experience different capital flows, labor requirements, life cycles, and economic, social and political environments.

Most major economic development events follow a common process. Each stage can be expected to influence the distribution of income and employment in the community in a slightly different manner. A general scenario of development will be presented in this portion of the paper. It will serve as the framework for analyzing previous empirical work.

Predevelopment

The first step in the process includes exploration, site selection, land survey, feasibility analysis, capital accumulation, property acquisition, preparation of impact analysis reports, and community reactions efforts, not necessarily in that order. For the developer this is perhaps the most important stage in the total process. It is here that most of the critical decisions determining ultimate profitability are made; millions of dollars are often spent in the process. On occasion nothing comes of the expenditure as the projections suggest a lack of profitability or the project is stymied by local political objections.

Although large expenditures occur in the predevelopment process, there is no assurance that they will immediately benefit the community. The exploration, surveys, capital accumulation processes, reports, etc. will probably be done by people external to the community with little money spent locally.

Nonetheless, the seeds for much of the ultimate economic distributional effect are sown at this time. Perhaps the most significant is associated with property acquisition. If the property purchased for the development itself is owned locally, then some of the capital may find its way into other local expenditures or developments. The specific site location chosen will, because of proximity, affect some people more than others. Changes in environmental quality and shifts in the movement of people will affect property values. Other examples could be cited. Thus, it is important to study predevelopment behavior when examining the distributional impacts of a major economic development.

Construction

The most visible economic shock to a community comes with construction of the physical facilities associated with economic development. Costs of idle capital are high, therefore construction is carried out on an "around-the-clock" basis. Some employment may be provided to existing residents; other workers are brought in. The latter may or may not live in the community. If many jobs require skills already present in the community's work force and thus go to locals, then one might theorize that their income would increase. If the jobs are unskilled, then low-income or unemployed workers might improve their relative income positions.

The workers and their families spend a portion of their income in the community generating further economic activity, primarily retail. Some new businesses may be created in response to the new opportunity. Much of their paycheck will go to taxes, insurance programs, health care, and goods and service imports, thus reducing the incomes to local businesses. It is also possible that the development may purchase some of its construction materials locally; this in turn creates secondary economic benefits.

When previously employed local residents are drawn into construction employment, their old jobs may or may not be filled. They may be filled by an underemployed or unemployed local, or by an immigrant. In either case, local employment increases. Often jobs in marginal firms are simply left unfilled. The individuals will probably be better off even though the number of jobs has not increased (Hushak, 1979).

A rapidly growing construction work force also leads to higher public costs. The increase in population, traffic, etc. will expand requirements for public expenditures for streets and highways, health care facilities, education and the like. Public expenditures require increased public revenues.

A rapidly expanding demand for workers is likely to place pressures on wage levels in existing jobs. This and demand pressures on limited community resources (e.g. housing, retail goods and services) will raise living costs in the community. Those unable to participate in the increasing benefits through higher-paying jobs at the development, or in secondary economic activity, sale or rental of property, will nevertheless bear the increased costs of living and higher taxes, thus being worse off than before construction began.

Operation

The long run impact of the major economic development event will be felt during its operation stage. In most energy resource developments the number of operating workers is significantly less than the number of construction workers (Shaffer and Fisher, 1981; Gilmore *et al.*, 1981). This may not be the case for other types of development (Kaldor and Bauder 1963).

The questions regarding the income distribution effects at this stage are essentially the same as those raised relative to construction. What skills are required? Who gets the jobs? How many new people move to the community? Who sells or rents their property? What new public services are required? What assistance is available from broader governments? Who gains, who loses?

The questions may be the same, but the answers are apt to be different. Many construction workers may be commuters, resident for only a short while. However, operating workers are more apt to become permanent residents. The effects are not only likely to be different, but surely more long lasting. It is the long run impact of major economic development that should be of greatest interest to residents of the community.

Shutdown

Many communities exposed to a major economic development will ultimately face its shutdown as well. Time may pass and perhaps the "newcomers" will become "oldtimers", but sooner or later the resource may be exhausted or the manufacturing plant become uneconomic, the defense installation may be closed, or the mine unable to compete.

A new set of questions arise. Who will leave the community for other employment? Who pays for public and private services and facilities left behind? One question remains the same: how are the costs and incomes of those who remain distributed?

Attribution

Before examining empirical research respecting the income distributional effect of any major development, we must note the difficulty of attributing measured change to a specific event. There is a wide range of explanations why income distribution may change over time (e.g. ability theory, human capital theory, theories of educational inequality, etc.) (Sahota, 1978). For example, individual income may change with a shift in national transfer payment policy simultaneous with a development event. As a result, personal income may be more equally distributed, but not only because of the development. Caution must therefore be exercised when linking changes in income distribution to new development (Reinschmiedt and Jones, 1977).

RESULTS OF PREVIOUS RESEARCH

There is much empirical research on the impact of major economic development events. Although little has been written specifically about income distribution effects, by piecing together the relevant bits of data a rational generalization of what usually happens can be constructed (Leistritz et al., 1982a; Leistritz and Chase, 1981; Rogers et al., 1978; Summers et al., 1976). In this section, those generalizations and the research from which they are drawn are cited.

Who Gets the Jobs?

There is very little research output regarding the predevelopment impacts of development projects; little can be said about who gets the jobs involved. It is probably safe to say that since most require relatively specialized skills, they go to permanent employees of the developing firms who are only temporarily in the community.

It is different when construction begins; many new jobs are opened. Generally they are filled with skilled younger men. "Younger workers are more competitive and flexible and, thereby able to take advantage of changing labor market conditions" (Deaton and Landes, 1978, p. 951). The areas in which projects occur are usually dependent upon agriculture or on a nondiversified economy. Young people have left for other income sources. The population remaining is thus older and less skilled. Thus, many of the jobs go to nonlocals. A recent study of energy-related developments in the Western U.S. found that locals held 40% to 60% of the jobs during the construction phase (Murdock and Leistritz 1979, p. 339).

Most of the nonlocal construction workers live outside of the community. A study of McLean County, North Dakota, indicated that less than one-fourth of the construction workers lived in the county during the construction of an electric generating station (Leistritz and Maki, 1981). They usually live in communities with populations in excess of 1,000 people but are apt to live in smaller towns than the operational workers (Murdock and Leistritz, 1979; Gilmore et al., 1981).

There is little opportunity for aged and unskilled workers during construction. Women heads of households, spouses and young unmarried females are also shut out of direct employment (Clemente and Summers, 1973a; Clemente and Summers, 1973b; Maitland and Friend, 1961; Black et al., 1960). The old, unskilled, and women may find increased employment in low-paying secondary jobs, usually in the service sector. However, there is little research to indicate the extent of this employment during construction.

During facility operations, a different employment pattern emerges. Direct jobs generally remain with skilled younger men, just as during construction. The percentage of the direct jobs which go to nonlocals remains large, but less than during construction. In a study of 254 cases of manufacturing development in the United States, an average of 30% of the plant workers were migrants to the community (Summers et al., 1976). Similarly, 80% of the operating workers in energy-related developments in the Western U.S. were locals (Murdock and Leistritz, 1979, p. 339).

The addition of new jobs may generate more permanent employment in the secondary sector as well. While local material purchases are generally small, a number of service sector jobs are created (McArthur and Coppedge, 1969; Mellor and Ironside, 1978; Gilmore et al., 1981). In the McLean County, North Dakota study, wholesale and retail trade grew by 22%; finance, insurance, and real estate 26%; and services 23% in a seven-year period. Each new direct job generated an additional eight jobs in the local trade and service sector. Two-thirds of the jobs were projected to be taken by locals. Most expansion occurred in facilities operated by local people or natives who had returned in response to business growth. In a four-year period there was a growth of only 5.5% in the number of firms (Leistritz and Maki, 1981, pp. 39-44). The conclusion that existing businesses gain most new sales was earlier demonstrated by Garth (1953).

The Summers et al. study of 254 manufacturing developments indicates a much smaller multiplier effect. Over half had employment multipliers of less than 1.2 (Summers et al., 1976, p. 55). This may be because McLean County is in a more sparsely populated region, its residents have fewer alternatives to expend their income.

Per Capita Income

Many studies have concluded that a major project generally increases per capita income in the host community (Davis, 1963; Bureau of Population and Economic Research, 1956; Gray 1962; Rogers et al., 1978; Murdock and Leistritz, 1979; Shaffer, 1974; Stevens and Wallace, 1964). In their massive study, Summers et al. found great variation in the increase in per capita income (from 5.3% to 183.0%) with over half experiencing an increase of less than 50%. Median family income increased less than 50% in about one-third of the cases. The largest percentage increases were found in those areas with the lowest average income prior to development (Summers et al., 1976).

A study of income changes associated with the construction and operation of 12 power generating plants produced similar results. In one case, total personal income rose by 28.1% but per capita income fell 1.5%. In the other 11 cases, increases ranged from 1.7% to 84.9% (Gilmore et al., 1981).

The introduction of 1,900 manufacturing jobs in Wynne, Arkansas, in the 1960s increased median family income 100.1% from 1959 to 1970, compared with only 56.2% for the state of Arkansas (Brady, 1974). In a study of industrialization in four counties in Eastern Oklahoma, Shaffer reports that all four exhibited an absolute increase in per capita income between 1960 and 1970. The average net income gain in the private sector was estimated at $3,314 per worker hired in the plant (Shaffer, 1974). In his study of the development of several firms in Searcy, Arkansas, Davis states, "Fuller employment in the manufacturing industries and higher hourly and daily wages in nonmanufacturing industries and higher hourly and daily wages in nonmanufacturing employment were primary directly contributing factors to the raising of per capita effective buying income..." (Davis, 1963, p. 42). A study of industry in Iowa concluded that the average monthly family income increased by over $150 after development (Paden et al., 1972).

Income Distribution

Those few studies which have looked directly at the question of productive for those who are able to participate directly. Negative effects may occur to others (Gartrell, 1982). The general consensus is, however, that overall community income is distributed more equally as a result of a major development event (Summers, 1973; Bureau of Population and Economic Research, 1956; Kresge and Siever, 1978; Mellor and Ironside, 1978; Rogers et al., 1978; Seiver, 1981).

Reinschmiedt and Jones reported a slight increase in income equality in their study of nine industrial plants in Texas. Individuals in the lowest income categories experienced the greatest income gain because many had been previously unemployed (Reinschmiedt and Jones, 1973, p. 71). Shaffer's analysis of industrialization in Eastern Oklahoma indicated a more equal income distribution as a result of development. In 1960, the lowest quartile mean income was 10% to 32% of the mean income; by 1970 it had increased to 28% to 50%, with an accompanying decline in the highest quartile (Shaffer, 1974, p. 101).

Individual Characteristics Affecting Income Impact

This section of the paper examines a series of factors which influence how an individual is affected by a major economic development event.

- Labor force status

In-migrants usually receive higher annual incomes than long-term residents. In a study of nine communities in which mining operations or military establishments were opened, income benefits are shown to be disproportionately obtained by new residents (Murdock and Schriner, 1978). In the Summers study of a rural steel plant in a relatively well-populated area, in-migrants controlled 12.2% more of the aggregate annual earnings than expected and the long-term residents 3.4% less than expected (Summers et al., 1976, p. 70). At the same time, it has been found that local workers who obtain employment at energy projects also improve their incomes substantially (Murdock and Leistritz, 1979). Although in-migrants tend to receive higher weekly wages than residents, there is some evidence to suggest that residents make greater improvement in their earnings (Olson and Kuehn, 1979). An analysis of industrial impact in six small Texas communities indicated that most workers increased or maintained their earnings when they took jobs in the plants. Once again, the unemployed and those with the lowest incomes prior to taking the jobs gained the most (Reinschmiedt and Jones, 1977). Conversely, a study of industrialization in the rural Ozarks showedthat more in-migrant heads of households experienced a loss of income than a gain (Bender, Green and Campbell, 1971).

A comparative study of two counties in Ohio, one with a plant employing 2,500 people, is more revealing. The median family income of a plant worker averaged $6,980 compared with $3,170 for all households. A population survey indicated that the young and those with a high school education benefitted most from the plant (Andrews and Bauder, 1968).

A plant location study in rural Mississippi helps to explain why in-migrant plant workers tend to earn the higher incomes. Plant workers received higher wages than others in surrounding rural areas, but the difference was explained largely by age and color. White open-country heads of households under 35 years of age had incomes about equal to those of the plant workers (Wilber and Maitland, 1963). Thus, if in-migrants tend simply to be younger than the average household head in the community, they will probably benefit most from the development (Murdock and Schriner, 1978).

- Age

Age appears to be a significant factor in determining whether an individual's income is positively or adversely affected by a major project. The construction of a large steel mill in rural Illinois had a negative effect on the relative income of the elderly residents of the community. In 1966 their median income was 0.396 that of the nonaged residents; by 1971, after industrialization, it had dropped to 0.339 (Clemente and Summers, 1973a, p. 481). The aged cannot compete with younger people in the labor market.

In contrast, Summers and Scott, writing later, reported that older persons increased their relative advantage during rapid development if cost of living changes are assumed to affect all age levels equally. Older persons reported a gain in income of 43.55% from 1966 to 1971. This compared with 21.47% for the 41-64 age group and 15.9% for the under-40 group. The closer to the new plant, the higher the gain for the elderly. This indicates that those who are able to capitalize on economic growth from a development event gain the most regardless of age. Those whose incomes depend totally on retirement benefits will be less well off (Scott and Summers, 1974). In another article, Summers and Clemente write that the effect of age on income inequality "is substantially mediated by sex, education, and labor force status...Age per se is not the major source of income inequality". They argue that income differences between strong and weak competitors tend to grow over time, and industrial development itself does not cause this. They conclude that the most important sources of income inequality are sex and labor force status (Summers and Clemente, 1976).

- Sex

There is some evidence that female heads of households receive little benefit from major economic development events. Historically, demand for construction and operations labor has been male dominated. The development may not worsen the female head of household's absolute income status, but does little to improve it. The only new jobs are in the secondary sector. However, this may be changing with increased public pressure to hire women in traditional male jobs (Clemente and Summers, 1973b; Mountain West Research, Inc., 1980; Vatne, 1982).

If a project does provide direct employment for women, the effect on family income is striking. A study of industrial development in Tennessee indicated that the principal influence on family income was associated with female workers taking jobs in the new industries. The number of families below the poverty line declined. In 70% of the cases, the change was aided by labor force participation of female family members (Deaton and Landes, 1978; Deaton 1979).

Cost of Living

A review of the income distributional effects of a major economic development event would be incomplete without examination of the distribution of associated costs. As Selvik has pointed out, "The absorption of a single energy development project in a community is the micro version of the macro problem of absorbing a new energy sector into a provincial or national economy. In both cases a demand shock may result..." (Selvik, 1982, p. 192). These demand shocks are not likely to be felt equally throughout the community. Although there is considerable research on changes in costs, particularly in the public sector, little is written on their distribution.

The introduction of a major activity which has a relatively high wage scale will have an early shock effect. The shift in labor demand forces employers to increase wages in an effort to attract an adequate supply of appropriate labor (Deaton and Landes, 1978; Leistritz and Maki, 1981). Not all employers raise wages, but enough do to influence the prices of goods and services in the community. In short, all costs of doing business rise. Local businesses find expansion more difficult and expensive. Ordinary goods and services are sought by a rapidly-growing population with little short-run expansion in supply. The cost of living increases for everyone, local and in-migrant alike (Murdock and Leistritz, 1979; Thompson *et al.*, 1978).

The rapid in-migration of construction workers and operations employees increases the demand for public services. Many public services and facilities may require costly expansion at about the same time. The project itself will place demands on the public sector. "New industry is clearly associated with an increase in the public sector costs of delivering basic services to residents (Summers *et al.*, 1976).

In most cases new development results in substantial increase in the value of existing property, residential, commercial and vacant properties alike. Most studies report increases in the assessable value of property in the community (Summers *et al.*, 1976; Garth, 1953). The opportunity for expansion in public revenue through increased property taxation is clear.

The increase in property value is a mixed blessing for many local residents. If they participate in the development and their incomes increase, the improvement in property value may be positive. If they are unable to participate, their taxes may increase without an increase in income.

The problem is compounded because the demand for public sector activities begins even before construction starts. The costs arise but increased revenues often come much later. Thus, even with the contribution of the new facility, the public sector costs may outweigh the benefits, especially in the short run. Residents may face a much heavier tax burden for some time. In some cases the development itself is not in the community's taxing district. In other cases it is not taxable (e.g. military installation). In both circumstances, the community is without taxing power. Often the firm or senior government will assist the community through predevelopment payments (Scott and Summers, 1974; Murdock and Leistritz, 1979; Leistritz *et al.*, 1982b; Leistritz and Maki, 1981; Gilmore *et al.*, 1981).

CONCLUSIONS

It seems quite clear that major economic development events generally cause the total personal and per capita income of the impacted communities to increase. Although there are few studies of income distributional effects, those that have been done report an increase in income equality. Either the proportion or absolute number of residents in the low-income category declines. Much of this may be attributed to the employment of the previously unemployed or the entry of women into the work force.

Development events are accompanied by a substantial in-migration of young, skilled, male workers, especially during the construction phase. The in-migrants may or may not live in the community. They receive much of the newly-generated wage income. At the same time they place demands on the public and private sector of the community. The prices of local goods and services increase and taxes may rise to meet increased public spending. In any case, the cost of living rises.

Major development events generally increase the property wealth of community residents. Storeowners experience increased sales while the demand for housing and buildings raises the value of local real estate. The wealth of certain individuals may be markedly increased through the sale of property at the site of the development. Nearly all of the research on income distributional impacts emphasizes wage income over other sources of income, thus the distributional effect of changes in wealth are unknown.

Some local residents gain from development through increased incomes. Others who are unable to participate in some way, are worse off. The elderly, female heads of households, and those who remain unemployed are most commonly affected adversely.

These observations account only for the more direct costs and benefits associated with a major economic development event. Development may create a number of externalities, for which no compensation is made. Examples might include environmental deterioration, and the loss of abundant wildlife and pleasing scenery. Power plants, mining operations, military bases, and large manufacturing plants are most apt to create such externalities (Nelson, 1979).

In a recent study aimed at including costs and benefits of all kinds, a sample of residents of McLean County, North Dakota (a coal and electric generation development) were asked if they thought their community was improving, staying the same, or declining. They responded as follows: 51.7%, improving; 36.3%, staying the same; 10.0%, declining; and 2.0% said they didn't know (Leistritz and Maki, 1981).

The income distributional impact of a specific major economic development event is thus determined by:

The relative size of the project in terms of employment and expenditure.

The nature of the event in terms of labor/job requirements.

The remoteness of the site in terms of the need for new housing and infrastructure.

The number of employees who live in the community.

The nature of the existing local population in terms of age, education, skill, sex, and current income.

The distribution of property ownership.

The political situation.

It is argued by some that ultimately the distribution of income is determined by political processes. Those locals who are the most powerful will determine who gets hired, whose property is sold, who receives capital for whatever purpose, and who gains access to other means to financial progress (Gartrell, 1982; Newby, 1982; Bloomquist and Summers, 1982; Gotsch, 1972).

The studies cited suffer a common series of methodological problems in terms of their value for understanding the effects of major developments on income distribution. Few deal with the question of income, much less its distribution. Most suffer from questionable attribution; they do not separate the income effect of development from the consequences of a multitude of other factors. Choosing a sample sufficiently large to appropriately control for all possible causal factors is all but impossible. When income is studied, annual income averages are used. These ignore inter-annual variations which may be substantial and tend to affect low-income people the most (Kuznets, 1955). None attempts to measure the net effect of the development event. None examines who gains and who pays the added cost.

Nonetheless, previous research does provide a rational approximation for what occurs with the development of mines, military bases, manufacturing plants, energy exploitation, etc. As such, its results provide some basis for informed choice by local, regional and national officials. There is a need, however, for much more specific knowledge if public policy is to have the desired distributional consequences.

Boom Towns:
The Social Consequences
of Rapid Growth

John W. Gartrell
Harvey Krahn
Tim Trytten
University of Alberta

The social impact literature contains a vividly-painted, widely-publicized stereotype of the socially disorganized boom-town (Kohrs, 1976; Gilmore, 1976; Cortese and Jones, 1977; Dixon, 1978; Albrecht, 1978; McKay, 1978; Davenport and Davenport, 1981; Wilkinson *et al.*, 1982). One of the better and more recent impact assessment handbooks describes this typical community:

> The new residents are frustrated by crowded housing (mainly trailers) and lack of amenities–especially recreational opportunities. Not surprisingly, these conditions aggravate family relations and lead to marital tension, child abuse and neglect, and delinquency. Wives are bored and husbands are under stress at work. Reported cases of depression, alcoholism, and attempted suicide greatly increase, as do mental health cases. Children have adjustment problems in school ... Community social pressure becomes less effective in controlling behaviour, including crime and delinquency, when the small, homogeneous community undergoes rapid development. (Finsterbusch, 1980; p. 141).

The interlocking problems of inadequate housing and community services, individual alienation, family breakdown, and minimal social control at the community level have been labelled the "Gillette syndrome" in reference to the experiences of residents of Gillette, Wyoming as described by Kohrs (1974). In western Canada, journalists have discussed, and residents of possible growth communities have feared, the similarly coloured "Fort McMurray syndrome". McVey and Ironside (1978) found that Fort McMurray was viewed as the least attractive place to live of all 17 Alberta towns with a population greater than 5,000. Yet despite these fears, the systematic empirical basis for this syndrome appears sketchy. Comments critical of its empirical basis have appeared elsewhere (Davenport and Davenport, 1981; Summers and Branch, 1982; Wilkinson et al., 1982) and it is not our primary focus. Also, methodological problems and issues of validity and reliability of measurement are not our principal concern. Instead, we:

1. Introduce several Canadian case studies in an effort to broaden the empirical basis of the debate.
2. Place this evidence within a conception of stages of development.
3. Develop a research agenda designed to focus the boom-town debate upon issues of broader sociological significance.

A SELECTIVE REVIEW OF
CANADIAN ENERGY RESOURCE TOWN RESEARCH

Drayton Valley, Alberta

Robinson (1962) focussed on town planning in Drayton Valley, a single industry community in the Pembina oil fields. It grew from a small farming community of 100 residents to a service centre of 2500 in less than two years. The lack of money for essential services handicapped efforts to meet the needs of the expanding population. Compounding the problem was the lack of training of members of the municipal government. Although Drayton Valley was a planned community, the swiftness of change surprised the planners.

This early emphasis on issues of planning and service provision parallels the central concerns in many contemporary studies of rapid growth towns. While there is less than adequate discussion of social structure changes, the demonstration that planning for rapid growth has advanced little in two decades is informative–and depressing. This case is also interesting in that a second boom hit the town in the late 1970's as a result of renewed drilling for oil. The consequence, again, was severe financial difficulty for the municipal government.

Fort McMurray, Alberta

Prior to large-scale exploitation of the Athabasca Oil Sands deposits in Northern Alberta, the isolated town of Fort McMurray was a small hinterland trading, trapping, and transportation settlement. Many of its small population were Indian and Metis, and underemployment was high. Construction of the two oil sands plants totally altered the physical and social complexion of the community. The social and economic changes, and the experiences of residents and migrants, have been documented in a long series of research reports.

Fort McMurray's contemporary economy is based on two large plants which extract synthetic crude oil from the oil sands. Prior to the construction of the first plant (Suncor), the town's population (1961) was 1200. By 1971, with the first plant in production, the population was about 6000. By 1982, four years after completion of the second plant (Syncrude), it had reached 32,000 and the town had become a city. Thus, the community has experienced two distinct construction booms during which housing shortages were acute, labour turnover was high, and social services were strained.

Matthiasson's (1970, 1971) survey of over 400 residents of the post-Suncor construction era documents reasons for migration (largely employment-related), mobility intentions (fairly short-term) and levels of satisfaction with aspects of community life (low satisfaction with labour-management relations and medical services).

Participant observation by two anthropologists (Van Dyke and Loberg, 1978) at the height of the Syncrude construction boom (1975) recorded unstructured interviews with 5 residents.

It is not safe to be too trusting because they are a different brand of people here. Like a frontier town in movies, people are tough, harsh, con men, drug addicts, and alcoholics (p. 74). The kids in town are being overrun with bad kids. The bad are overpowering the good (p. 77). The primary problem here is mistrust between people. It is now a town of strangers stepping on each other and cutting each other's throats (p. 91). Nobody I know here is happy with their family life. I don't know if it is due to long hours of work and shifts or not. There is a lot of cheating and unhappiness (p. 93).

Such are the many volunteered comments which suggest that the disruption of rapid growth was being felt in 1975. However, this research report also contains many positive comments about life in the community.

If you can get out and meet one person in this town, chances are you break into a small circle of friends (p. 72). Fort McMurray is a good place to hide from relatives. We were having a lot of problems with in-laws, so we had to get away from them (p. 78). McMurray has helped our marriage. We were having serious problems that were money oriented. With the increased income, our problems are decreasing (p. 94).

The Gartrell et al. (1980a) survey of 430 randomly-selected adults focusses on the demographic characteristics, experiences, behaviours, and attitudes of residents in Fort McMurray in the post-Syncrude construction era. In 1979, it did not appear to be a problem-ridden, grossly under-serviced community where everyone endures primitive conditions to make a "fast buck". Yet the popular conception is correct in some ways. Household incomes are high, 25-20% greater than those in Alberta, as were standards of living. The community had experienced rapid population growth. It contained a high proportion of males and the young. Turnover was high although some stabilization appeared to be occurring. The labour force had a high proportion of those with relatively unstable employment histories, and residents had histories of high levels of geographic mobility. Residents were relatively dissatisfied with some aspects of their lives; e.g. the quality of their neighborhoods, the external design of their housing.

This is only a partial picture, although the population may be young and mobile it also contains a high proportion of families. Fully 76% of adults were married or lived common-law. The proportion of residents who expect to make Fort McMurray a permanent home doubled to almost 50% between 1969 and 1979. There is little evidence of either conspicuous consumption or severe debt. Some improvements in housing supply have been experienced and compared to Matthiasson's results (1970, 1971), service quality appears to have improved.

Residents of Fort McMurray report that they are satisfied with their friendships, family life, jobs, economic circumstances and they are optimistic about their financial future. The level of associational affiliation is no lower than the Canadian norm. Residents are no less integrated into neighbourhood or friendship networks and they do not feel more alienated than do residents of Edmonton, a much larger, rapidly growing, city. Residents reported (Krahn et al., 1981) their own marital satisfaction to be high, yet 55% viewed this community as one in which marital infidelity was high and 72% thought family breakdown was common. The negative reputation has lingered although construction and rapid growth have abated.

There was, therefore, little evidence that rapid development had widespread negative psychological effects on the residents of Fort McMurray during this period. This does not prove that Fort McMurray is a city without problems or that rapid growth and high mobility do not have social and personal costs. It does demonstrate that energy resource communities change and mature, that people can adjust, and that various organizations can be instrumental in facilitating this adjustment.

Grande Prairie and Peace River, Alberta

Fort McMurray is not the only energy resource community of importance in northern Alberta. Grande Prairie and Peace River, situated in the northwestern agricultural region, have both received energy-related development projects. Grande Prairie has grown dramatically into a community of around 25,000 as a consequence of gas drilling. Peace River remains smaller but will also grow rapidly if a proposed dam and several oil sands plants are built. The available studies of Peace River (Nichols and Associates Ltd, 1981) and Grande Prairie (Carcajou Research Ltd., 1980) are typical of commissioned social impact studies.

The Peace River pre-impact study relied on official information to describe the restricted employment possibilities and the demographic characteristics of the population resident in the region. The relatively low level of public service provision and the probable consequences if the inadequacies are not reduced, are identified by referencing the experiences of Fort McMurray during its construction boom. Policy suggestions include "erring on the high side" in projections of demands and the development of flexible service provision programs. This study, then, offers useful pre-impact aggregate data, some typical policy-related planning suggestions, and virtually no sociological analysis.

The Grande Prairie study also provides aggregate data on population growth and on service and housing demands. The methodology of this study consists of unstructured interviews with residents and agency personnel (N = 379 in total) along with reliance on official data and participant observation. The problems of specific groups which have felt the most negative consequences of rapid growth (e.g., the elderly, single parents, renters) are emphasized. Although its range of information is broader and its methods are more varied than the Peace River study, it remains a largely theoretical report with an emphasis on social services and social interaction.

Cold Lake, Alberta

A 10-12 billion dollar heavy oil extraction development had been proposed for the Cold Lake region of northeastern Alberta, but a combination of political and economic factors have recently stalled construction. The approximately 25,000 people in the region live in three towns, three smaller villages, two Indian reservations and several Metis settlements, a large military air base of almost 6000 or on farms (20%). A study of the region was undertaken in 1979 (Gartrell et al., 1980b) in an effort to map its socioeconomic features prior to project impact. The methods employed were similar to those used in the Fort McMurray study (Gartrell et al., 1980a), and a total of 1,166 interviews were completed in addition to a survey of business establishments.

The 1979 survey of residents revealed a highly stable, socially well-integrated population. As with other rural areas, education levels, household incomes, and labour force participation rates were below provincial averages. Incomes, employment rates, and levels of living were particularly low in the Metis Settlements. Satisfaction with housing, services, and the quality of life in general was high. The construction of a heavy oil extraction plant would bring few direct opportunities for local residents but would create significant opportunities in the service sector. The elderly on fixed incomes would be likely to benefit little, while those who owned property stood to gain a great deal. The experiences of Indian and Metis residents in other boom areas suggest that they would also benefit little from development. Respondents' opinions about the proposed development appear to match these predictions. A majority stated that they favoured development but few thought local residents would benefit. Instead, oil companies and local businesses were considered most likely to benefit. Many respondents were concerned about in-migration of "transients" and "undesirables", and about inflation.

Cartwright, Hopedale, and Sageak, Labrador

Using a "moderate dependency theory" House (1980, 1981) describes experiences of off-shore oil and gas exploration. Based on two summers of field work and extensive personal observation of the political, social and economic aspects of off-shore development, he concluded that, although oil and gas development may represent an historic opportunity for this region to develop, albeit in a dependent manner, there has been little benefit to the region to this point.

The interests of the multi-national oil companies (growth and profits) could, but have not, meshed with the interests of local residents. Residents operate in a pre-industrial "social economy" where economic matters are imbedded in kinship and other social relations. The "occupational pluralism" of the coastal villages might fit very well with the flexibility preferred by the industry, but few jobs (and those low-paying and unskilled) have gone to local residents. Local entrepreneurs have not benefitted, since the oil game is much too capital-intensive. Thus, small Labrador communities felt social disruptions of various kinds (this research was published prior to the Ocean Ranger disaster) but received less than average benefits from resource development.

The House research is unique in that it begins and ends with sociological theory. It does not emphasize the presentation of empirical data and does not examine the experiences of in-migrants to the region. While identifying some familiar themes in the literature (e.g. locals benefit least), its strength lies in the theoretical framework which guides the discussion and encourages further comparative research.

STAGES OF DEVELOPMENT

Although the literature on Canadian single-industry communities contains descriptions and even typologies of the stages of development of boom-towns, the fact that these communities will probably mature and eventually decline has not been considered in much detail. Finsterbusch (1980, p. 138) notes typical construction, operations, and shut-down stages, reports that expected impacts do not always occur, and briefly discusses the "boom-bust" phenomenon. Still, the boom-town literature emphasizes the present and the past. Comparisons of the observed present to the (usually unmeasured) past allow the "Gillette/Fort McMurray syndrome" to remain strong. The negative impacts do occur. The issue remains one of documenting their prevalence, their expansion and contraction, and their determinants. In short, what are the typical stages of development of relatively isolated single industry communities?

Available typologies differ in detail, but the basic descriptions are similar. First, there is a discovery and exploration stage. Developers and entrepreneurs of various types become involved in the local economy along with the resource development firm. The highly unsettled, booming construction period follows. Migration and labour turnover are high, and social services, housing and community facilities may be inadequate. In the operations phase, the labour force contains more young, skilled and less transient workers. The original residents may become a minority in the new town. Families are more likely to be attracted to the community, and housing, social services and urban amenities begin to approach an acceptable level. If the economic base of the community is maintained, the population will approach a more typical age-sex distribution. Finally, as we are witnessing with increasing frequency, a final stage for some single industry communities is their sudden decline following a plant shut-down.

Recognition of the manner in which single resource communities develop and change allows us to predict that the level of social disruption would increase during construction and then begin to level off during the operations phase (Figure 1). Presumably, disruption would decrease as the community matured. Whether the level of community disruption after the boom is similar to that before is an open empirical question. Other hypotheses suggest that the size of the construction and operations workforces may increase social disruption. The sophistication of the technology employed may have an effect on social disorganization via the selective recruitment of workers. Government intervention in the construction and planning of the new or changed community presumably has an effect on the height of the curve, as may policies of financial compensation, local hiring and selective recruitment. The characteristics of the town's major employer (absentee owned, multi-national, etc.) may affect the social organization of the community, particularly through planning strategies and willingness to invest in community infrastructure. All of this, however, remains hypothetical. The comparative research remains to be done.

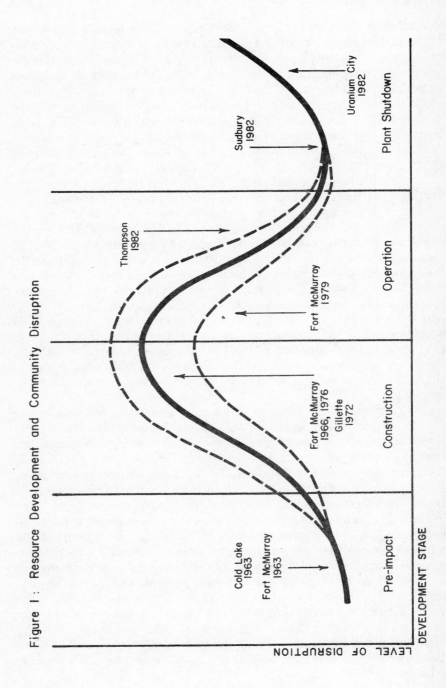

Figure 1 : Resource Development and Community Disruption

Looking at Canadian communities, for example, we might see Cold Lake, Alberta in the pre-development stage. Fort McMurray in the mid-sixties and again in the mid-seventies exemplifies the disruptive construction phase, and Fort McMurray in 1979 was moving into the less tumultuous operations phase (Figure 1). Communities like Sudbury, Ontario and Thompson, Manitoba are in the mature stage and in the current recession show symptoms of severe decline. This graphic presentation of changes in the level of individual, family and community problems allows us to incorporate both "boom" and "bust" into our discussion. An extremely high level of social disorganization/disruption may occur if the town's primary industry folds. Uranium City, Saskatchewan, which recently lost its primary industry, is a recent example of a community socially disrupted as a consequence of a "bust."

TOWARDS A RESEARCH AGENDA

There has been a tendency in this literature to lament the absence of sociological theorizing, particularly at the community level, while contributing none. Furthermore, there appear to be two basic value-orientations in the boom-town literature. The first, the pessimistic approach (Champion and Ford, 1980, p. 26), centres around the "Gillette/Fort McMurray syndrome" and links major developments to social disorganization within the community and personal problems for its residents. This orientation is challenged by the optimistic perspective which interprets the boom as an opportunity for community expansion and diversification. The boom may produce some social disorganization but will result in economic growth and a brighter future. In addition:

> For most development areas, population growth has been a long unfulfilled goal. The loss of young adults, as a result of undiversified economies and heavy dependence upon an agricultural base with an ever-increasing level of mechanization, has led to older populations, lower income levels, and low rates of overall population growth and has produced areas that generally require growth in order to stabilize their basic infrastructure. (Murdock and Liestritz, 1979, p. 65).

This hope does not apply, of course, to the development of isolated new towns.

What might distinguish between these two orientations is the discipline of the researcher. Like the blind men describing the elephant, each sees only a portion of the whole beast. The economist will document the employment and multiplier effects, the sociologist may study value differences, community integration and attitudes towards change, and the planner may be horrified by the crisis management styles of local officials. Optimistic or pessimistic appraisals of the boom-town are, in part, a product of the issues examined.

Central to most of the negative assessments of large scale developments is the emphasis on rapid population growth. This "people pollution" (Gold, 1979) is frequently assigned a primary causal role in the sequence of social and economic changes (Gilmore, 1976; Albrecht, 1978; Little, 1977), since fewer people would mean fewer problems. In effect, this may be an unconscious form of "blaming the victim" since it would be equally appropriate to identify the original cause as a location decision by a corporation or the failure of government and industry to plan adequately. Whatever the case, the consequences of heavy in-migration are clearly identified in this literature.

These consequences include value conflicts between old-timers and newcomers (Nellis, 1974; Little, 1977; Gold, 1979) flowing from different lifestyles or the differential demands for specific services. In the latter case, the conflict may be aggravated by the old-timers' belief that newcomers will not remain in the community to help pay for the new services. Unequal benefits from development (e.g. more and better jobs for in-migrants) are noted frequently. Particular groups such as the elderly, farmers, or the uneducated are often identified as especially vulnerable. Finally, housing inadequacies and the need for temporary housing, service overloads, and high population turnover are also central topics in these studies.

There are also some systematic omissions from the boom-town literature. As mentioned earlier, sociological theory at the individual or community level is seldom introduced to such studies. Most research remains at a descriptive level. There is minimal recognition of the stages of community development and of the many factors which might affect social organization and the quality of life during these different stages.

The attractiveness of boom-towns lies in their employment opportunities. Yet there is very little known about the experiences and rewards of work, about the labour markets which migrants leave and which they enter in the boom-town, and about the relationships between workers and employers in these communities. While we cannot remedy all of the omissions in this literature, we can suggest some avenues of sociological research related to working in an energy resource town.

One possible research route is suggested by the review of House's (1981) study of Labrador communities. His emphasis on dependency theory places the impacted community in the context of a larger world economy. The local effects of development, including the lack of jobs for local residents, are linked to international processes of capital accumulation, dependency and uneven development. Bradbury (1979) presents an extensive theoretical framework with the same emphasis. Clement's (1978) discussion of regionalism in Canada emphasizes the same large themes. This global top-down perspective complements the following general discussion of community factors related to resource development. Both approaches are useful and necessary. We have simply chosen to focus on the community level rather than on its political-economic context in seeking explanations for the impact of the community on the behaviour of its residents.

Community Parameters

In social, economic and political terms, large scale energy resource projects have different effects under different conditions. If no community exists, "new towns" are created. If a small isolated community already exists and is expanded to host new workers, its social structure is radically altered. Larger pre-development populations, less isolation, government intervention, and smaller, multiple or more slowly phased in projects condition the social impact of development. In any case, the social relations of production in the dominant industry determine the social relations and basic class distinctions in the community. Yet descriptions of social impacts are remarkable for their consistent omission of class structure.

Local class structures vary with the degree to which industry management elites are resident in the community. Ownership is generally absentee (Lucas, 1971; Clement, 1978). Other segments of the regional or national elite (politicians and civil servants, developers and landowners, commercial leaders) may also be largely absent. The community's existence and well-being are generally in the hands of outsiders. Hence, local class structures are likely to be attenuated at the top. They also contain a variable representation of petit bourgeoisie, this class being larger if the initial population was larger. This group includes local businessmen, landowners, developers and others, who may have profitted from the boom, as well as farmers or ranchers whose class position is based upon a different mode of production (sometimes dominant before the boom). The class structure most certainly contains some white-collar managerial, professional, and administrative personnel, other white-collar workers (clerical, retail) who are not in command of others' labour, and blue-collar workers. In addition, the class structure would encompass those no longer employed (retired), the unemployed, and perhaps some members of indigenous (native) communities. The latter, however, are of indigenous (native) communities. The latter, however, are often physically segregated, poorly integrated into the capitalist economy and often heavily dependent upon public sector institutions.

A first research step would be a detailed mapping and a cross-community comparison of the class structures of energy resource towns. Then we can begin to assess the differential impact of development on different classes within (and outside) the community. Further research might examine levels of class consciousness, class conflict in various forms, and the changing social relations of production within the dominant local industries. Class consciousness research might benefit from comparisons to the "affluent worker" research in new towns in Britain undertaken by Goldthorpe *et al.* (1969). The Kerr and Siegel (1954) hypothesis about workers in isolated industries being more likely to strike (Bulmer, 1975) might be useful in examining class conflict. Clement's (1981) study of Inco in Thompson and Sudbury is an example of research focussing on the labour process and the changing nature of labour-management conflicts in single industry towns.

In addition to class distinctions, the social organization of the single industry community is generally segmented by differences between core (the resource company) and periphery sectors. Housing markets and residential areas may be segmented along parallel lines, particularly where major companies provide housing in efforts to reduce turnover. Social network formation may be heavily conditioned by this physical aspect of economic segmentation.

Beyond class structure and segmentation, four key demographic factors further condition the community's experience of rapid growth: the size and composition of migration, birth, sex, and marital status cohorts. For example, new and old housing is likely to be segregated and neighbourhood composition may be dependent upon when settlement occurred. Such differences are often compounded by differences in age composition of residents (newcomers are younger) and differences in lifestyles. Social organization is furtherinfluenced by marital status, with a large number of single males in the town, particularly during the construction phases. Finally, labour markets are segmented by sex and women may experience difficulty in getting good jobs; employment opportunities may be largely in peripheral sector firms.

Again, important questions await research. Do different migration cohorts participate unequally in the social and economic costs and benefits of development? What are the unique characteristics of life in the construction camps? Goffman's (1961) writing on "total institutions" might be a useful introduction to such research. Some initial work on construction camps associated with North Sea Oil development has been undertaken (Moore, 1981), but there is nothing comparable available for

North American energy resource communities. There is persuasive evidence that women have restricted employment opportunities in resource towns, but the extent of discrimination and the mechanisms through which this inequality is maintained have not been thoroughly examined. Further research might focus on how household labour is divided and traditional sex roles are maintained in male dominated communities (Luxton, 1980).

An Attainment Model for Energy Resource Communities

Two major life events, migration and job change, provide an individual-level biographical perspective to asess the opportunities provided by energy resource communities. We can assess the impact of these life events, and through them the impact of development, within an appropriately modified status attainment model. This approach emphasizes that:

1. individuals are linked through occupations to the structure of production and situated within a class structure;

2. jobs are the principal reason why people move to or remain in these communities;

3. employment opportunities are a major benefit which resource development claims to bring; and

4. the use of individual biography to add the time dimension to impact assessment.

Employment opportunities thus provide a focus for the evaluation of the social impact of development. This perspective is generally lacking in the studies reviewed above and in recent social impact assessments in Canada and the U.S.A. (Bowles, 1981; Finsterbusch, 1980).

The status attainment model views respondents' present positions as a function of their social origins and other "ascribed" status factors, education, and experience. It thus models individual biography, focussisng upon occupational prestige or income as the outcome of the attainment process. In a boom-town, an additional factor-the impact of resource development-must be introduced. Status prior to migration (or prior to the advent of development), as well as origin characteristics, are viewed as exogenous. Thus, for in-migrants, status and status change prior to moving provide the relevant base, while for old-timers, pre-development status is the comparable base. The opportunities provided in a resource community become an additional predictor of current status or income. In other words, do such communities allow newcomers and original residents of the area to "get ahead"?

Given the differences in employment opportunities at different stages of development, the timing of migration (length of residence) and job change are probably important covariates. Timing of job change might also be relevant for the original residents, who could be included as a separate cohort in such an analysis. Preliminary elaboration of the model, beyond specifying status before and after development, would include separate analyses for these different cohorts. In order to incorporate social class and the segmentation of local labour markets into core (primary) and periphery (secondary) sectors, status attainment analyses should also compare labour force segments and social classes. We might expect that different migration cohorts, social classes, and labour market segments would exhibit different pay-offs in status and income attainment. Comparisons of community status attainment parameters could be made across resource developments to evaluate the relative opportunities provided by boom-towns. For example, Marchak's (1979) study of the British Columbia timber industry suggests that status attainment possibilities are limited and that only in the higher technology areas are education, occupation and income related. Similarly, local estimates could be compared to estimates from larger national samples.

Status Attainment in Fort McMurray

This kind of analysis has been undertaken in Fort McMurray (Krahn and Gartrell, forthcoming). Analysing occupational prestige for a sub-sample of 193 currently employed males, we found only marginally greater mobility in the boom-town than in a comparable national sample. More detailed examination of the data revealed several interesting findings. First, frequent and substantial changes in socioeconomic status accompanied the move to the community, and this involved both downward and upward mobility. Those who obtained jobs in core sector firms benefitted most. Of those employed in core sector firms, 37% had moved up, 17% had moved down, and 46% had stayed the same. In periphery sector firms, 22% had moved up, 34% had moved down, and 44% experienced no status change after the move.

Second, there was strong support for the hypothesis that migration to Fort McMurray offered a way out of periphery sector employment. Almost half (49%) of those who left periphery sector employment when migrating found core sector employment. Only 14% of those who began in core sector firms moved to periphery sector firms in Fort McMurray. Third, while workers in core and periphery firms were equally likely to have been unemployed before moving to Fort McMurray, those in the core were much more likely to have had a job pre-arranged. If not, they still reported less difficulty in obtaining employment. Finally, men employed with the oil companies were able to translate their previous occupational status and experience into destination status at higher rates than men employed in the periphery. In sum, the advantages of energy resource development for migrants were concentrated in the core sector.

Whether this project provided greater mobility opportunities than other projects cannot be ascertained without data from other communities. The relatively small proportion of women employed in the core sector (about 13%) and the few original inhabitants of the region even resident in the community in 1979 (3 out of 430 in our sample), clearly indicate that these groups have benefitted less than male in-migrants. Larger samples of women and indigenous residents are needed to document this process. Finally, class differences in status attainment remain to be examined. Classes could profitably be disproportionately sampled in future research, largely because of the high proportion of working class residents in this community.

Selective Migration and the Quality of Life

The composition of the social collective is altered by selective migration both to and from the community. Our conception of the process of social impact specifies that migrants bring with them certain capacities and inadequacies which, in turn, are affected by the existing social milieux. Individuals may bring their own problems and success but, to some degree, their experiences are also shaped by the social organization of the community.

One way to improve our understanding of the relationship between people's social position in boom-towns, and the problems which they experience and perceive, is to split social status into three conceptual parts. The first part can be accounted for by charateristics which occur before the impact of development (or before migration): origin status, sex, age, ethnic status, I.Q., education, and pre-move occupational status and income. These pre-impact characteristics represent selection factors and could loosely be referred to as "ascribed" social statuses. The second component of present status can be attributed to post-impact situational characteristics that describe community effects: life events, housing and employment. This would include that part of current status which was a function of migration cohort, social class position within the community and segmentation in local employment. Finally, a part of current status is composed of random error and systematic factors which have not been explicitly included in the previously noted determinants of status. This third component (the systematic variance) represents what could be loosely described as "achieved status". Residual status scores would represent current achievement net of what could be predicted on the basis of origin, education and situatiional community factors (Turner and Gartrell, 1978).

Disaggregation of current status into these three components, employing regression techniques, would yield three variables. They could then be related to a variety of quality of life measures, problems, and attitudes towards the community. This would allow the assessment of which components of current status influence personal outcomes. Furthermore, as suggested above, these effects could be compared across cohorts, social classes, and segments within the community. One community could be compared to others, and estimates of community parameters could be compared to results from more general samples.

CONCLUSIONS

Looking back over the research agenda, it is obvious that the state of the art in the study of energy resource communities is rather primitive. Despite the many academic studies and social impact assessments, we know little about the influence of resource development on the social organization of small isolated communities. Large subject areas, particularly occupation, class structure, and status attainment, need research. The introduction of relevant sociological theories would clearly improve the social impact literature. Also, there is clearly benefit in broadening our investigations to include consideration of the impact of developments of all kinds (Summers *et al.*, 1976).

In conclusion, we must emphasize the importance of longitudinal research, or at least comparisons of communities in different phases of the development process. We know little about turnover within these communities and, thus, about the degree to which problems and successes are exported with out-migrants. Assessment of the social impact of development cannot be satisfactorily completed without such studies of movers and stayers. In order to understand social organization in energy resource communities, comparative designs must be used to isolate and identify selection factors that determine the composition of boom-towns. Knowing this, we might have more success in untangling the effects of the boom-town social environment on the lifestyle and life-chances of residents.

Votes Count,
But Resources Decide

Gene F. Summers
Leonard E. Bloomquist
Department of Rural Sociology
University of Wisconsin-Madison

It is the objective of this paper to provide a "state of the art" summary of what is presently known by social scientists of how spatial decentralization of economic activities, accompanied by centralization of control, affects the structure of power and dynamics of influence within localities. While attempting to avoid being drawn into the vortex of the ideological debate of elitism versus pluralism, we will draw upon community power structure studies for evidence. We will rely upon case studies of communities which have been coping with large-scale economic development since these situations provide heuristically valuable "laboratories" for observing the processes of power.

THEORIES OF COMMUNITY POWER STRUCTURE

If it were possible, it would be desirable to avoid the use of the term "power" altogether because of its vague and inconsistent usage. However, the term cannot be avoided and it is therefore essential that we attempt to construct a conceptual schema for our review. Power is a hypothetical construct used to describe observed patterns of dominance in relationships among two or more actors, where actors may be individuals, organizations, collectives, or even entire communities or nations. These attributions appear to rest on one of three elements or facets of a relationship: (1) the ownership or control of resources, (2) the use of resources, and (3) the outcomes of resource utilization. While definitions of power are many and various, they have an essential meaning which posits power as the ability to control a situation so as to produce a desired outcome, or at least to increase the probability of desired results, even in the face of opposition.

Despite an awareness of the importance of all three facets of dominance, theories of community power structure vary in the locus of their emphasis. Some theoreticians look upon the ownership and control of resources as the inter-group difference to be explained. While perhaps tacitly assuming that the pattern of ownership and control ultimately affects outcomes through efficient utilization, there is little attention to power use or outcomes. Some of the early, descriptive case studies of community power structures follow this pattern (Mills and Ulmer, 1946; Hunter, 1953). Ownership of economic resources and/or official political office-holding is described, whereupon it is assumed the "elitist power structure" of the community has been delineated and the mobilization of those resources to further self-interests at the expense of others is accepted as an inevitable consequence (Banfield, 1965; Long, 1958, 1962; Walton, 1967).

At the other extreme are theoreticians who turn their attention to the pattern of issue outcomes in communities, particularly policy outcomes (Hawley, 1963; Banfield and Wilson, 1963; Wilson and Banfield, 1964; Crain and Rossenthal, 1967). While there often is an explicit recognition of the importance of resource ownership and utilization, the emphasis is placed upon issue outcomes, their patterning over time, and identification of whose collective interests are served by the pattern of events (Mansfield, 1963; Dye, 1968; Hage and Aiken, 1967; Mohr, 1969; Alford, 1978; Aiken and Alford, 1974). To some extent is appears this theoretical emphasis on outcomes is a direct reaction to the earlier emphasis on resource control (Clark, 1967, 1968).

Asis so often the case in the history of ideas and theoretical fads and foibles, alternatives exist long before interest fades and dissatisfaction emerges into the open, or at least they co-exist and receive scant attention until the fad is found wanting. The record of community power research is an example.

By the time frustrations with the structuralists' "comparative urban studies" approach began to surface, there already were studies underway which focussed more directly on the dynamics of the political processes within communities. They addressed the question of "who gets what, when, where and how". One might note that the structuralist style came into vogue with: (1) the dissatisfaction of social scientists with the power structure methodological and ideological debate, (2) the emergence of computer technology which permitted huge amounts of data to be assembled, analyzed and re-analyzed with little cost in time or money but which also forced the researchers to have little or no first hand knowledge of communities being analyzed, and (3) the explosion of Federal programs under the Kennedy and Johnson administrations, to assist communities in dealing with poverty and other racial and ethnic inequalities.

The end of the 1960's was also the end of innocence. It was quite understandable that liberal social scientists were beginning to systematically investigate political realities in search of answers to the questions of "how these policies came into being" and "who really benefitted from them". By the mid-1970s there were numerous program evaluation studies dealing with the politics of policy impacts (Kramer, 1969; Crenson, 1971; Hayes, 1972; Greenstone and Peterson, 1973; Alford, 1974; Fainstein and Fainstein, 1974; Rossi, Berk and Edison, 1974; Wirt, 1974; Miller, 1975; Warren, 1975; Summers et al., 1976). At the same time there were European scholars developing theories of inequality which attempted to place local politics (especially urban) into a broader regional and national context) e.g. Castells, 1972, 1973; Harvey, 1973; Newby, 1977; Pahl, 1971; Pickvance, 1976; Williams, 1973).

In this large, growing and somewhat chaotic body of literature, we find an explicit treatment of the fact that extra-local decisions regarding resource utilization may affect the entire community rather than merely segments of it. There is also a tentative conceptualization of the processes by which communities sometimes act for their collective welfare (Tilley, 1973).

CASE STUDIES OF LARGE-SCALE DEVELOPMENT

Communities which host large-scale economic developments, willingly or otherwise, are recipients of capital investments controlled by absentee owners with extra-local organizational ties. Usually, these communities also receive substantial numbers of immigrants. These circumstances afford social scientists an opportunity to learn a great deal about the processes of community social change. But social scientists are not the only interested parties, as is attested to by the growing social impact literature. Private industry is also willing to sponsor monitoring projects, and Federal and State governments are supporting research aimed at mitigation. While the interests of participants in this conference are focussed on energy resource communities, our review of case studies is not limited in this way. It is our presumption that the basic processes of change stimulated by and associated with large-scale economic developments are likely to be similar regardless of the type of economic activity involved in the development. Even if this premise is incorrect, we can only discover that by including all case studies at this point in our review.

The case studies reviewed were restricted, however, in several respects. First, the case studies had to be empirical analyses of community change either concurrent with the development (monitoring studies) or reconstructions of events after the fact. Impact projections were not regarded as case studies. Second, the economic development had to involve about one thousand or more new jobs within a restricted time (up to three years). Third, the community had to be relatively small in population prior to its development experience. We used the U.S. Bureau of the Census definition of "nonmetropolitan" as a "rule of thumb" to define the domain of small communities. Fourth, the authors had to make an explicit analysis of resource ownership and/or control, resource utilization for collective actions on behalf of interest groups (not necessarily the community as a whole), or the outcomes of resource utilization. Of course, the authors need not have employed these terms, since they reflect our preference for a descriptive and analytical framework. Most researchers used terms such as "power structure", "interest groups", "conflict", "participation", or just simply "politics". We did insist, however, that case study authors make some conscious and deliberate attempt to analyze political behaviors in order for us to incorporate their study into our review.

Case Studies of Large-Scale Development

Author & Date	Location	Type of Development
Present, 1967	Southern California	Defense Contract Mfg.
French, 1969	Northeast Illinois	Auto Assembly Plant
Lucas, 1971	Rural Canadian communities of single industry	Manufacturing, mining, mills and railroads
Laumann, Marsden & Galaskiewica, 1977, 1978, 1979	West Germany & Central Illinois	High Technology R & D and State University
Dixon, 1978	Fairbanks, Alaska	Alaskan Pipeline
Seiler & Summers 1979	Central Illinois	Steel Mill
Hooper & Jobes 1982	Ashland, Montana	Mining and Electric generating plants
Pijawka, Albrecht & Branch, 1982	Salina, Utah	Mining
Wilkinson & Thompson, 1981	Craig, Colorado	Electric Generating plants
Albrecht & Bergmann, 1982	Price, Utah	Mining and electric generating plants
Branch, 1982	Douglas, Wyoming	Mining, oil refinery, electric generating plants
Branch and Bergmann, 1982	Grants, New Mexico	Mining and electric generating plants
Hooper & Branch, 1982	Forsyth, Montana	Electric generating plants & mining
Thompson, Kimball & Williams, 1982	Rangely, Colorado	Oil Shale
Williams and Thompson, 1982	Wheatland, Wyoming	Electric Generating Plant
Fredenburg, n.d.	Paonia, Colorado	Mining

When these selection criteria were applied jointly, the pool of case studies was reduced dramatically. Our insistence that the authors must have examined an issue of community power was the main source of pool reduction. Table I provides a brief guide to the case studies which were examined in detail and which form the data base for the inferences presented in the next section of the paper.

GENERALIZATIONS

These inferences are arranged into three groups: (a) Pre-development, (b) Development and (c) Post-development.

Pre-Development

1. Ownership and/or control of economic resources is such that some residents own none and, among owners, shares are usually concentrated. Thus, an economic elite can be identified among residents. However, there are exceptions to this tendency which are significant.
2. Ownership of means of production is an important basis for membership in the resident economic elite, where these resources include land, capital, and industrial plants and machinery.
3. Ownership of commercial establishments is another important basis of membership in the resident economic elite.
4. There is an apparent potential (and sometimes real) conflict between these two segments of the economic elite. In rural communities this often appears as a town-ranch (farm) clash.
5. Control of political resources is contingent upon ownership of economic resources.
6. Knowledge of local economic and political matters is contingent upon membership in the local elite group because of the informality and personal character of interactions.
7. There are interactions among those who own and/or control economic and political resources to an extent that a network can be identified which constitutes an organizational resource, although it is often in an incipient form.
8. Local marriage markets are restrictive and therefore resident owners of economic and political resources often are kinsmen by birth or marriage.
9. Many, perhaps most, economic and political transactions among residents are executed informally and interpreted by the actors as personal relations.
10. There is a general acceptance of the belief that among residents,

shares in the ownership of locally based resources bears a direct relation to one's stake in the welfare of the community. This legitimates economic resource owners' dominance in the control of political resources and their use of them for the collective interest of other resource owners–to the extent such action can be justified to other residents as being in the "community's interest".

11. Resident owners of locality-based resources perceive the future security of their investments as dependent upon the general welfare of the locality and therefore often act to further the "community's interest".

12. Resident owners of economic resources in the secondary and tertiary sectors usually perceive the future security of local investments as dependent upon the welfare of the local export sector and often defer to it, especially in public policy matters.

13. Resident ownership and control of resources within a locality usually are associated with non-local interactions involving counterparts in other localities and respresentatives of extra-local organizations. These interactions generate knowledge and organizational resources external to the locality which often are used to influence local actions of benefit to collective interests.

14. Communities vary in the extent to which local economic resources are owned by residents. Even in pre-development communities one can observe cases where an absentee owner controls a large segment of the local economic resources. Absentee owners may be individuals, investor-owned corporations or senior governments.

15. Non-resident owners of economic resources may avoid direct participation in local politics when their economic interests are not involved. In this circumstance the politics of local welfare issues and concerns are left to residents, creating a bifurcation of power, or perhaps an illusion of non-involvement. On the other hand, non-resident owners may elect to use their economic resources to control virtually all political informational and organizational resources in the locality, as in the case of some company-owned, single industry towns.

16. The non-resident owner's freedom of choice in local affairs is largely a function of the role played by senior governments through legislation and administrative policy affecting rights and obligations of local governments and private firms.

Development

1. Large-scale economic developments invariably involve capital investments controlled by non-resident owners and investors who sel-

dom have direct involvement in or knowledge of their firm's activities in the host community. Often the investor/owner is another corporate entity rather than a person. Thus, decisions are made by professional management personnel.

2. Management personnel of development agents–corporations and senior government–make decisions regarding local activities within a context involving many factors in addition to locality considerations. The security of their firm's investments and their careers are tied primarily to extra-local organizations and the outcomes of sequences of events beyond the local arena. This is in sharp contrast to resident owners.

3. Management personnel of development agents often are more knowledgeable about the workings of non-local business and government than local economic and political leaders. The manner in which this knowledge superiority is used becomes critical in the adaptation of the host community to development.

4. Where large-scale development involves massive expenditures of money in the local economy and immigration of workers, especially during construction, the host community must deal with a rapidly expanding economy and increased demands for public goods and services. Thus, resident economic and political leaders must make many decisions in an unfamiliar situation requiring knowledge, management skills, capital, physical facilities and organizational resources which they often do not possess or control. Moreover, the future often is very uncertain and largely beyond the control of local leaders.

5. During development, the importance of several non-economic and non-traditional political resources as determinants of local events become apparent: (a) knowledge of business and governmental matters beyond the local setting, (b) advanced management skills, and (c) tactical use of organizations, locally and non-locally. While possession and use of these resources by local economic and political figures may have been adequate for pre-development circumstances, large-scale growth conditions often demand quantities of them and a level of competency in their use which exceeds the ability of local leaders. Thus, the increased significance of these resources poses a real challenge to the owners of pre-development resources; especially since newcomers often hold a competitive advantage in the newly valued resources.

6. Reactions of pre-development economic and political leaders to the unfamiliarity and uncertainty of growth appear to be based largely on personal ideology and philosophy. Some local leaders adopt a short-run "profit-taking" orientation which maximizes the gross

receipts to costs ratio in business and in government. Others assume a long term "investment" orientation which allows short-run costs to be amortized over a longer term and de-emphasizes short-run profits.

7. Local leaders' reactions to their inadequacies in knowledge, management and organizational skills vary considerably and quite independently of their "profit-taking" versus "investment" orientation. Some leaders turn to private consultants or hire professional managers and planners. Others turn to senior government agencies or the development firms for information and guidance, while still others postpone decisions and attempt to rely upon their own resources.

8. The expenditure of large sums of money in the local economy and population growth often cause the incipient clash between town-business and rural-farm and ranch interests to become explicit. For the owners of businesses and real estate and/or equity capital, growth promises a rise in net profits. For farmers and ranchers, especially those whose land is not suited to real estate development, growth promises a reduction of net profits. Thus, political opposition between these collective interests frequently surfaces during development.

9. Large-scale development creates role conflict for resident economic and political figures. The opportunity for personal economic gains is no longer seen as being equated with the community welfare. To the contrary, public policy decisions leading to greater community welfare may actually reduce or restrain the local opportunities for owners of economic resources. Faced with this role conflict, some economic and political leaders withdraw from political activity (at least publicly visible activity).

10. Growth increases the aggregate disposable income which causes changes in organization and operation of local markets for goods and services. Many who possess the increased income are not owners of other economic or political assets. Thus, as a collectivity with primarily a consumer interest, the non-owners (workers) gain ability to influence community events, albeit an unorganized and uncoordinated collective interest. Pre-development residents often experience this as a newly gained freedom of choice in shopping for goods and services.

11. During development, organized interest groups sometimes form and demand action on matters of common concern. These mobilization efforts are usually issue specific and seldom represent a challenge to the resource base of the pre-development leaders. Issue mobilization most often comes from widespread person inconvenience and

comfort. Occasionally it comes from a violation of the local norms of equity when benefits are unfairly accruing to one person or group. In rare instances, mobilization comes from an ideology at variance with that of the local leaders.

12. Newcomers with knowledge, management skills and extra-local organizational ties represent a greater potential challenge to existing leaders than other newcomers. This applies in both economic and political sectors. Seldom is their challenge a matter of public mobilization. Rather it is made by exercising their competitive advantage in the daily course of business.

13. Senior governments provide capital through loans and grants, technical assistance for planning, and legal instruments through legislation. They control enormous resources which intervene in the local influence processes. The interventions of senior governments affect private sector resource utilization in the local economy as well as local political decisions. However, the extent to which representatives of senior governments become visible participants in local economic and political decision-making varies nationally and regionally within nations. In the United States, senior governments generally exercise their local influence by providing resources only under specified conditions. Thus, senior government intervention appears to affect the autonomy of the local state and the local economy more than it affects the distribution of resources among economic and political actors within the locality.

Post-Development

1. The stability of the pre-development distribution of economic resources and their utilization is a negative function of the size and rate of large-scale economic development. By definition, large-scale projects interject new economic resources into the local economy and, in doing so, alter the distribution of ownership and control.

2. Where the addition of economic resources is accompanied by immigration, a separation of economic and political spheres of influence occurs. Whereas pre-development political resources were contingent upon economic resources, post-development political resources have a more diverse origin. In particular, pre-development dominants seldom possess the technical knowledge, management skills and organizational ties necessary to deal effectively with public issues of growth. Newcomers, hired professionals, senior government representatives, and the development firm's representatives who possess these resources have a competitive advantage. Their participation, either publicly or unobtrusively, alters the structure of power

in the political sphere and encourages a separation of economic and political powers.

3.   The tendency toward separation of powers notwithstanding, pre-development influentials may be able to retain much of their previous power by enlisting the services of professional managers and planners, either as employees or consultants. The success of this strategy, however, depends on local leaders' ability to control the professionals.

4.   The instability of power which accompanies development sometimes can be reduced by senior government actions to place growth management instruments at the disposal of pre-development leaders. Legislation to strengthen the legal and institutional resources of local government bodies appears to be the critical element, although it needs the additional support of technical and fiscal assistance.

5.   Ultimately, the stability of pre-development economic and political power rests with the non-resident owners and managers of resources in the private and public sectors. The economic and political resources introduced by development usually overwhelm the locally-owned and controlled resources. Local leadership stability depends largely on the disposition of the development project management and senior government personnel to maintain the integrity of local leadership. At the one extreme are the company-owned towns and government reservations. At the other are communities where existing leaders are provided with resources and allowed to manage the growth process within limits imposed by the external powers.

6.   The democratic processes of citizen participation may function, but only within constraints. In the words of the Norwegian political scientist, Stein Rokkan, "Votes count, but resources decide".

Impact of Resource Development Projects On Indigenous People

Charles W. Hobart

Department of Sociology,
University of Alberta

INTRODUCTION

In the past, the impacts of resource development projects have been disastrous for indigenous populations and communities in many parts of the world. At a minimum native peoples were progressively stripped of the lands necessary to their livelihood (Bodley, 1975). Often, governments colluded with industrial interests in attempts to coerce local indigenes through the imposition of forced labour, or head taxes, poll taxes and hut taxes which were designed to force native people into wage employment to earn money to pay the taxes (Hutt, 1934). A more subtle approach involved raising consumption levels among native peoples, so that they came to need or want a variety of trade goods, which they could obtain only by earning money (Bodley, 1975).

When these systems did not work for one reason or another, there was always the simple expedient of kidnapping workers. Such "black-birding" was common for the half century preceding 1910 in the South Pacific: Melanesian natives were taken by force and sold to plantation owners in Australia and elsewhere in that area. In some parts of the world it has simply been more convenient to kill off indigenous people because only their land and its resources were wanted.

Canadian history is not free of such incidents, as the extermination of the Beotuk Indians illustrates. More commonly, the Hudsons Bay Company, as well as the other trading interests, had a policy of motivating native peoples to trap furs by stimulating their interest in trade goods. Aboriginal peoples have been extremely vulnerable to many forms

111

of exploitation and the involvement of native people in development activity has often been involuntary. We should remember the kind of "softening up" process to which native people in Canada have been exposed prior to their more recent actual involvement in development projects.

This paper is concerned only with Canadian and primarily northern Canadian examples, because these are the cases I know best, and because it is necessary to reduce the long list of possible inclusions in some way. Following a brief overview of the industrial work experience of native Canadians before 1965 I turn to a discussion of three alternative resource development scenarios and their consequences for native communities and native people.

NATIVE EMPLOYMENT PRIOR TO 1965

Generally it must be said that the attitude of Canadian industry toward employing native people has not been enthusiastic. These people have typically been seen as disinterested in the kind of work available, undependable and given to high absenteeism and high turnover rates. At northern work sites, where the active work season is often quite limited and deadline pressures are heavy, such workers have been seen as an added source of uncertainty in a work environment where there are far too many such sources already. Imported southern white workers were seen as more reliable, and the only way to dependably get the job done.

Before the mid-1940s the attitudes of native people in northern areas of Canada were complementary to those of industrialists; most native people had little interest in industrial employment. They preferred their traditional lifestyle and hunting and trapping made this lifestyle financially feasible for most. In northern Canada generally, this situation persisted until the end of World War II when the fur market collapsed and the cost of trade goods rose suddenly. The result was an economic squeeze which stimulated a lively interest in wage employment among many native people that continues to the present day (Cohen, 1962; Helm and Lurie, 1961).

The first effort to involve native people in an industrial operation on a significant scale occurred between 1958 and 1962 at the nickel mine at Rankin Inlet in the Northwest Territories. Early efforts to operate the mine using an all white work force proved to be fruitless because of very high turnover rates. A consultant recommended that Inuit (Eskimo) workers be hired and a 70% or more Inuit workforce successfully worked the mine until it closed in 1962, following depletion of the ore body. Inuit workers were found throughout the operation, including some in very responsible positions such as mine plumber and mine electrician.

Very few of these Inuit were native to the immediate area. The majority were from Coral Harbour, Chesterfield Inlet and Whale Cove. Many of the latter were minimally acculturated Cariboo Eskimo from the inland regions of the Keewatin who had survived the starvations of 1957 and 1959 and had been evacuated by the government to the coast. Accommodations at the mine, in the form of very small houses, were supplied by the government to the "starvation camp" survivors in a camp about a mile from the mine site. However, most of the Inuit were not so fortunate, and had to improvise such huts and shacks as they were able to build from materials scavenged from the mine dump (Williamson, 1974).

While the Inuit became very effective workers underground as well as in the mill, the shop and on the maintenance crew, this adaptation was not accomplished without difficulty. Some workers found it almost impossible to obtain adequate rest in their tiny, noisy houses during the periods of 24-hour daylight. During the season, Inuit were accustomed to visiting and other activity around the clock, stopping to sleep when the need overcame them. Workers suffered and many dragged themselves to work in very run-down condition. Often their wives did not know how to plan a meal using store bought foods, and some on occasion were observed returning from the store with only candy to feed their families. Absenteeism and tardiness were problems and the company became increasingly insistent on punctuality, hiring a local Inuit to try to make sure that workers arose on time in the morning. One indication of the anxieties that Inuit workers experienced in trying to meet company expectations is seen in the fact that some were found to be wearing two wrist watches (Williamson, 1974).

The Rankin Inlet Nickel Mine Inuit employment experience demonstrated the industrial labour capabilities of Inuit when working with management who were appropriately appreciative of Inuit capabilities. This was so despite the difficulties of the local situation in which the Inuit found themselves: makeshift shacks or government housing that was too small and greatly overcrowded, too little comprehension of how to adjust to the commercial and town-like environment in which they found themselves and certainly too little assistance in helping them to adapt. Yet adapt they did, and even the presence of a beer hall at the mine site offering unlimited access to Inuit did not lead to widespread drinking problems. Accordingly, while it must be said that many Inuit experienced considerable initial difficulty in making the transition from their semi-traditional inland or coastal living patterns to those appropriate to an industrial community, they did adapt successfully and within a surprisingly brief period.

In retrospect it is clear that despite its unpromising aspects, the Rankin Inlet mine situation had most of the necessary components for a successful industrial employment situation for the Inuit. The mine management was generally favorable, alternative work forces having failed. The mine manager was formerly the consultant who recommended employing an Inuit work force. He had the trust and loyalty of the Inuit, he knew how to work with them, and the Inuit badly wanted the employment. Some from Chesterfield Inlet and Coral Harbour had some prior industrial work experience in connection with construction of the air strip at Coral Harbour during World War II and some of the DEW sites during the late 1950s. The survivors of the Keewatin starvation camps were demoralized and disoriented in the coastal camps to which they had been relocated, since they knew nothing about the hunting of sea mammals. Inuit throughout the north were suffering from the depressed condition of the fur market following World War II. In this situation, mine employment offered a dependable source of quite adequate income, at least in the short run, and with motivation thus assured, the pragmatic adaptability of the Inuit asserted itself.

The most unfortunate aspect of the Rankin Inlet mine employment was its short duration. Inuit were not hired until 1956 and the mine closed in 1962. A survey conducted among the Inuit employees after the closing date was announced, showed that almost all of them wanted more industrial employment. Only 14% said that they wanted to go back to trapping and living on the land (Williamson, 1974). The Department of Indian and Northern Affairs made efforts to place them in other mining situations, and a few were relocated to Yellowknife, Lynn Lake Manitoba or to Arctic Quebec. Most returned to the areas from which they had come, where they were again dependent on hunting, trapping, and welfare payments. Thus, for most, the mine employment experience only briefly opened a door to a new solution to the problem of survival.

Inuit employment experiences were not always so fortunate, however, as another case suggests. During much of the 1960s the Department of Indian and Northern Affairs instigated efforts to involve Inuit workers at the Asbestos Hill mine in Arctic Quebec. Information on this experience was obtained from the mine manager, who was candid in his description of the situation. Management did not want the Inuit, anticipating that they would be unsatisfactory workers. The other workers at the mine, French Canadians, did not want to work with the Inuit, complained that "they stink", and refused to room with them in the mine bunk house. Finally, the Inuit said that they did not want to work there, that they had "plenty of money", and that they were only there because they were pressured by Indian Affairs. Clearly the factors making for success at the Rankin Inlet mine were absent here. A thoroughly unpleasant situation developed which eventually resulted in abandonment of this native employment opportunity.

In recent years, wage employment in development industries has become much more accessible to native people in the Canadian north. It has become available in three contrasting contexts, which typically have different consequences for native people and for industry as well. Where the work site is easily accessible to the worker's home he may move daily between the two, as do most workers in the south. If employment is not accessible, the worker may relocate with his family to the distant work site. Finally, the worker may rotate between his home and a distant work site, living for a time in each place. In the remainder of this paper, the consequences of each of these alternatives for the worker, his family and his community, and for the industry which employs him are discussed in the light of recent examples.

WORK SITE IN THE HOME COMMUNITY

Where the work is located in the home community, that community is typically a southern-style town, such a Yellowknife, Hay River, Inuvik, 300 person Frobisher Bay, or Pine Point. It is not a native settlement, even a large native settlement such as Rae. The native people living in these towns have already made the choice of living in a situation essentially dominated by southern Canadians and their culture. The influences experienced by these workers and their families derive largely from this urban setting, rather than from the features of the industry in which they are employed.

Where an industry has moved in and built a company town, as at Grande Cache in Alberta and Faro in the Yukon, the local native settlement, where such existed, has typically been thrust aside. The effects on the native community derive largely from the very rapid establishment of a southern town, rather than primarily from the industrial employment in which a few local native people may be involved.

Two clear examples of northern Canadian situations in which energy resource developments have located near a native community are the Suncor and Syncrude plants situated near Fort MacKay in northeast Alberta, and the Dome-Canmar marine drilling base at Tuktoyaktuk in the Northwest Territories. Unfortunately, neither of these situations is adequately documented. In the case of Fort MacKay, it appears that few residents of this very small settlement (population of about 200) were much interested in either construction or operations phase employment with Suncor. This was no longer true when the Syncrude plant was built, and a number of the Fort MacKay men did work intermittently on this construction project, and somewhat fewer have worked during the operations phase. At least one major reason for this sparse involvement was that transportation to the plant site 20 km distant was not provided for Fort MacKay workers, as it was for workers living farther away in Fort McMurray.

Fort MacKay has undoubtedly suffered from proximity to the oil sands developments. It lost traditional berry-picking grounds, game has been scared away from some areas, and it has experienced pollution of air and water. It occasionally suffered indignities and intimidation at the hands of adventure-seeking construction workers during the Syncrude construction phase. There has been conflict within the community, but this may be related to the diverse band composition of the community and difficulties in adapting to a more settled lifestyle, as well as to issues posed by the proximity of industry. The community has experienced much less conflict than has Janvier, a native community in the same region which is much more isolated from industrial employment. While there are liquor problems in the community, there are no indications that these are worsening any more rapidly than in other native communities in Western Canada.

The effects of the Dome Canmar operation on Tuktoyaktuk, an Inuit community of about 800 people, have been much greater. This is the staging site for Dome's steadily increasing Beaufort Sea drilling operation. In the spring of 1981, Dome built a 300-person base camp which is filled to capacity during the summer and fall drilling seasons. The most visible impact has been the economic effects of the Canmar Drilling program, which generated about $3,000,000 in 1980 or about 55% of the total community income. By contrast, fur harvest and social assistance payments comprised only 1% each of the total. During the 1980 drilling season 149 Tuktoyaktuk residents worked for Dome or its contractors, earning a total of about $1,100,000 (Outcrop, 1981).

The social impacts are more difficult to specify precisely. There has been increased alcohol consumption, but this is generally true in Arctic communities. Fur harvests have not declined. There are local complaints that Dome small-craft in Tuktoyaktuk harbour scare away fish, disturb fishing net-sets, and endanger native people crossing the harbour in small boats. People have been observed shaking their fists at the Dome aircraft, often seen flying near the hamlet.

Dome has worked hard with the community to try to prevent some of the most obvious adverse social impacts. The base camp is kept liquor and drug-free by a vigorous policy of searching the baggage of all people traveling to the camp and discharging offenders when they are discovered. In response to an early wish of the Tuktoyaktuk Hamlet Council, the settlement was declared off-limits to non-local base employees, and offenders are dealt with promptly. It is obvious that Tuktoyaktuk residents have reaped rich financial rewards. It is also apparent to one having long familiarity with the community, that since 1976 the very rapid growth of the Canmar operation and the related employment have imposed severe strains on the community. The community currently appears to be coping, but the level of tension is high. The proximity of many influential whites at the base camp is clearly disruptive to a traditional native community.

RELOCATION WORK SITES

Employment experience at work sites to which employees relocate with their families is not very common among native workers. Until very recently, most industrial employers had little confidence in native people as potentially dependable workers. Since relocation work sites typically involve some subsidization of the worker, employers have preferred to make this investment in white workers whom they felt were more reliable.

A number of Fort Chipewyan (Alberta) residents, with their families, were involved in relocation employment during the construction of the Syncrude oil sands project north of Fort McMurray. Some were able to rent lodgings in Fort McMurray, some moved in with friends, and some 'squatted', camping in the bush in the vicinity of the town or the plant. During the course of interviews with 16 people in Fort Chipewyan, I encountered only one who reported favorably on the experience of these relocating workers. The cost of food was high, accommodations were not to be found or they were exorbitantly priced, and people disliked living in an obviously "white town" after having spent most of their lives in their own Indian community. The result was that after a short time most moved their families back to Fort Chipewyan. It is clear from the interviews that the high cost of living and the experience of a white-dominated town were particularly important reasons for their return.

The second example involved relocating Indians to a well appointed company town where they were provided attractive accommodations. During the early 1970's the management of the Sherritt Gordon Ruttan Lake Mine at Leaf Rapids, Manitoba entered into an agreement with the Department of Indian Affairs to relocate the families of suitably skilled Indian employment recruits to the Leaf Rapids town site. This relocation program was well funded and the Indian families were given the same accommodations as others in the town. Two counsellors were provided, one to assist the adjustment of Indian workers on the job, and the other to help in the social adjustment of workers, wives and children in the town. Every attempt was made to facilitate integration and to forestall any adverse community reaction, and these efforts were quite successful.

However, in discussions with the counsellors it was learned that while the workers typically had little difficulty in adjusting to their jobs, their families and particularly their wives often were not happy. As a result, they often returned to the Indian communities from whence they had come, forfeiting the opportunity for wage employment.

The root of the difficulties experienced by such families is often the feelings of alienation and estrangement which many native people experience when they move from the native reserve or settlement to a white community. In place of the easy and frequent contacts with the extended kin group and the comfortably familiar patterns of settlement life, natives in town are thrown in with whites who may commonly be distant, patronizing, or unmistakably rejecting. The feelings they may experience were poignantly expressed by the wife of an Inuk who with others had relocated his family to Roma Junction, Alberta while he was employed on the Northern Alberta Railroad. In drunken despair, she blurted out to an Inuktitut speaking anthropologist, "There is no place for me in this land" (Stevenson, 1968).

Native men in these situations may be somewhat more acculturated, and may achieve relatively good work adjustments if they are not distracted by the difficulties that their families are experiencing. However, a very important element in the self concept of many native men, particularly those who have been raised in more traditional communities, is their identity as a hunter who keeps his family supplied with wild meat. This feeling of obligation is strengthened by the preference of family members for traditional foods. It is usually very difficult, if not impossible, for native men to combine successful worker and hunter performances in a relocation work setting.

The experience of the families of a dozen Inuit workers who were relocated to the company town at the Nansivik mine site on northern Baffin Island illustrates some of the problems. These families came from relatively small traditional communities around Baffin Island: Igloolik, Clyde River, Pangnirtung, and one or two from more distant settlements, such as Gjoa Haven. The men performed excellently at their jobs in the mine or the mill, to the complete satisfaction of their foremen. The families lived in modern, suburban style houses with all of the expected conveniences, and these were appreciated. But the little community of Nansivik, with a population of 280 in 1980, is unquestionably a *white* community. The Inuit families missed the independence they experienced in their own Inuit communities. They felt out of place, and they missed their kin groups. The mining company made a significant concession in providing release time for Inuit workers who wanted to go hunting, but these men encountered an unexpected difficulty. The northern Baffin Island terrain is very rough and mountainous and none of the relocated men were native to the area. As a result they found that they simply could not hunt seriously for fear of getting lost, a very significant consideration (Baffin Region Inuit Association, 1979).

ROTATION EMPLOYMENT

Most of the industrial employment experience of northern native people in western Canada has involved rotation employment, where the worker alternates between home and work site, spending one or more weeks in each location. The duration of the work period differs, from as little as four days, to as much as six weeks. The major disadvantage of this type of work schedule, of course, is the separation of the worker from his family and his community. There is no doubt that work periods in excess of three weeks induce significant stresses, particularly when associated with long work days (Baffin Region Inuit Association, 1979; Hobart, 1976). However, by now there is much experience with native employees working such schedules, with satisfactory results in every case.

The most successful of these work experiences involves the Gulf Minerals uranium mine at Rabbit Lake, Saskatchewan. This mine is operated by two complete work forces, each of which works 80 hours during the course of seven days, and then spends the next week at home. The workers are primarily farmers from the more northerly farming areas, and Indians from four or five northern reserves. All those hired are selected very carefully in order to minimize worker turnover. All are trained for at least semi-skilled employment levels, and are encouraged and rewarded for learning alternative skills.

This approach to rotation employment has been remarkably effective. The most dramatic indication has been the very low turnover rate among native employees of only 5% per year from 1976 to 1979. The work performance of native workers has been equally gratifying. Finally, the self-assessment of the four communities which supply native workers seems to indicate that the rotation employment has had no significant adverse effects on workers' home settlements (Beveridge and Schindelka, 1980).

Similar patterns are found in rotation work projects in the Northwest Territories, where the most common schedules involve two weeks at work and one week at home, or two weeks at work and two weeks at home. The most thoroughly studied of the Territorial rotation employment programs is the experience of an Inuit village, Coppermine, where between 54 and 90 men were employed by Gulf Oil Canada drilling operations between 1972 and 1979. There were some transitional difficulties during the first year, which were ascribable to the lack of prior industrial experience among all but a very few of the Inuit workers. At the work site there were a few incidents of damage to vehicular equipment because the Inuit did not understand the importance of preventive maintenance. In the community there was a significant (29%) increase in alcohol consumption and an increase in drunken violence, directed primarily against eight wives who apparently were suspected of infidelity. However, at the end of the drilling season the company felt that the program had been a success, and a survey conducted in Coppermine showed that over 80% of the workers and the workers' wives felt that the employment experience had been a good thing, and wanted the worker to again have this employment (Hobart and Kupfer, 1973).

During the next two or three years, these problems virtually disappeared. The Coppermine Inuit became some of Gulf Canada's most effective and dependable workers. Liquor consumption and drunken violence levels fell below those found before initiation of the rotation employment. There was no indication that children suffered neglect, or that returning workers spread illness. The seven-day rest periods at home gave workers adequate time to hunt, and the fur harvest appears to have increased. Oil company earnings enabled workers to buy more skidoos, boats and other equipment so that they became more efficient (Hobart, forthcoming).

Similar consequences appear to have resulted from the two-week work rotation schedules established by Pan Arctic Oil's High Arctic Drilling Program, by Dome Canmar's Beaufort Sea drilling program, and by Esso Resources in its Beaufort Sea drilling and Norman Wells refinery operations. The effectiveness of the native workers has tended to vary with the opportunities made available to them. Gulf Oil had a much stronger emphasis on worker upgrading than Pan Arctic Oil, and has experienced comparably better worker performance. Inuit may make a somewhat more rapid and enthusiastic adjustment to rotation industrial employment than the Indians of the Middle Mackenzie (Fort Norman, Fort Franklin and Fort Good Hope), who comprise the native workers at the Norman Wells refinery. Even in the Middle Mackenzie, however, my own recent data suggest that there are increasingly positive reactions to the rotation employment (Roberts, 1977; Hobart, forthcoming).

Dome Canmar has striven consistently to increase the size of its native work force and to expand the number of jobs at which northerners are employed in its Beaufort Sea drilling program. It has achieved remarkable success and the proportions of native workers who remain on the job until the end of the drilling season have increased substantially. Although the drilling program in the Beaufort Sea is opposed more or less bitterly by all of the native organizations, native workers are typically enthusiastic about working for Dome Canmar and speak very positively about its employment policies (Outcrop, 1981; Hobart, forthcoming).

A somewhat different picture emerges when one turns to work programs involving longer work rotation schedules. Among Indians employed by Hire North to learn operation of heavy duty equipment and to help construct the Mackenzie Highway, there were some who liked the 30-day work period, saying it was a relief to escape from the liquor-related problems of their home communities. However, the training supervisors reported that they could see the increased stress in many of the workers towards the end of their work periods. Tempers became shorter and the trainees became more difficult to supervise.

These difficulties are even more clearly demonstrated among the rotating (as distinct from the relocated) Inuit workers at the Nanisvik lead-zinc mine, who have a six-week work period. Particularly eloquent is the fact that about one third quit and went home before completing their first six-week work period. Only 57 % of all the Inuit employed between 1975 and 1978 actually completed their first six-week work period, while no more than 27% remained Nanisvik mine employees for more than two work rotations, i.e., more than four months. The reason for these early terminations was home-sickness in virtually every case (Baffin Region Unit Association, 1979).

The feelings of the men were matched by those of their wives at home, who encountered other difficulties. Many experienced shortages of meat while their husbands were away. Moreover, since the traditional attitude was that food is primarily wild meat and money is spent for hunting equipment and consumer goods, men often did not make arrangements to have money forwarded to their families. As a result, some wives found themselves out of food and out of money as well. In addition, many of them found their children difficult to control while their husbands were away, and some were troubled by unwanted attention from other men during their husbands' absences (Baffin Region Inuit Association, 1979).

The result of these circumstances was that 42 percent of the Inuit employed at the Nanisvik mine from 1975 to 1978 were young, unmarried men. Married men became increasingly unwilling to subject themselves and their families to the privations and the hardships which the six-week work period imposed. This points to the social regressiveness of rotation employment programs involving long work periods. They select young unmarried workers and bring relatively high earnings to the people who are least responsible, have the least need and are most likely to spend excessively on alcohol, drugs, or in other non-socially productive ways. At the same time, such workers tend to be the least stable on the job, perhaps because they lack the family responsibilities which make for a stronger commitment to satisfactory work performance (Baffin Region Inuit Association, 1979).

SUMMARY, CONCLUSIONS AND IMPLICATIONS

Following the collapse of the fur market shortly after the end of World War II, native people became very eager to obtain wage employment. Despite the official pronouncements of native organizations to the contrary, in most areas this interest continues to the present (Hobart, 1982). Indeed this interest has grown, as the concentration of the native population into a relatively few centres, the rapid increase in the native population, and increased educational attainments have made traditional sources of financial support less accessible or less attractive. This paper has presented information on three different patterns of development employment for native people: where it is available in the worker's home community, where it involves relocation of the worker with his family to a home at the industrial work site, and where it involves rotation employment. In most cases it is rotation employment which is the least disruptive.

There are several important reasons why industrial employment in the worker's home community is not desirable. The many and powerful non-native personnel who must staff such an operation swamp the native community, so that it becomes increasingly white contaminated if not white dominated. Equally serious, in the long run, the attractive and prestigeful role models with which the children of the community will identify will be white people, or natives who are particularly successful in the project. A native community which served to transmit native language, values and traditions may lose its independence and its traditional identity, coming increasingly to promote English facility, southern values and southern lifestyles. The fact that men working on the project will find it very difficult to keep their families adequately supplied with game and to maintain their traditional game-food sharing responsibilities will tend to further accelerate this process. The freedom from family separation which this industrial scenario provides is purchased at a very high cost to community independence and continuity of the traditional culture.

Development projects involving relocation of native workers' families to the work site have the significant advantage of insulating their home communities from direct contact with the southern white influences. The disadvantages here accrue to the worker, to his family, and to the company operating the project. Wives are cut off from relatives and friends at home and may soon come to feel "there is no place for me here". In addition, the worker has his own difficulties in fulfilling expectations as "meat provider" and making a place for himself on the job. Typically, the inflexibilities of his work schedule will not make available adequate blocks of time for him to meet his provider responsibilities. Even where this is not the case, unfamiliarity with local terrain may make it difficult for him to provide game food, and leave him feeling that he is failing as a "true Inuk".

The result of these tensions is likely to be that before many months have passed the worker quits and moves his family back to the home community. The consequence for management is a dissatisfied native work force which is prone to quitting suddenly in an area where replacement hiring may be very difficult.

Rotation employment appears to avoid these difficulties if the length of the work period is no more than two weeks. The costs of such work-imposed separations should not be underestimated, but they are familiar to many native families which have seen men depart on long hunting and trapping trips. The close-knit nature of native communities, and the strong patterns of sharing and mutual assistance probably enable most native families to cope better with such absences of the husband than would be the case in white communities.

The most significant advantages of rotation employment, paradoxically, involve protection of the workers' home communities from white influences, while maximizing the ease with which novice native workers may be socialized to become dependable and effective workers. Native home communities are protected because the only link between the community and the industrial project is the worker. No other industry-induced white influences invade the community. Natives typically experience living in the white work camp as stressful and they are only too glad to immerse themselves in the distinctively traditional aspects of their community life when their work rotation is over. Far from influencing them to overvalue a white lifestyle, their experience at the work camp tends to enhance their appreciation of the traditional life they experience at home. This tends to "innoculate" their children against any too-ready tendency to idealize the southern lifestyle.

The socialization advantages of rotation employment for novice native workers lies in the fact that while at work they are in a completely controlled environment. Problems which are endemic among many native employees who work in their home communities include tardiness and absenteeism, induced by late drinking parties, the irregular hours which long periods of 24 hours of daylight or of "dark time" encourage, and the absence of a well-developed work ethic. By contrast, the native worker at an industrial work camp finds that the activities of his fellow workers, and indeed all of camp life, rotate around the work schedule. A novice worker at the camp tends to be locked into the same schedule as his fellows, retiring, getting up, going to work, eating, etc. at the same time that others on his shift do. Failure to go to work on time or missing work entirely thus becomes virtually impossible, except when the worker is ill. In this way, familiarization with the industrial work setting and good work habits are acquired with minimum difficulty or effort.

Rotation employment also allows any disruptive effects of this new work experience to be spread geographically to a number of different settlements. Similar benefits of rotation employment on drilling platforms have been experienced in Norway and Scotland.

Some rotating workers are able to have some of the best of both worlds. With the exception of Banks Island, native people in the Canadian north are typically not able to support themselves through hunting and trapping alone. Successful resource harvesting requires expensive equipment such as skidoos, boats, outboard motors, guns, and camping equipment. Thus hunter-trappers must subsidize their preferred lifestyle with wage employment. Work rotation employees earn the money to keep themselves supplied with new equipment, and they have the necessary frequent blocks of time to hunt and trap. Their success as hunters and as workers tends to assure them high status in their home communities, and their successful integration of modern and traditional forms of employment ensures their continuing involvement in both. Commitment to a more traditional lifestyle by those well-respected in the community is crucial to survival of the traditional culture.

These considerations lead to an important conclusion. Assuming that the work period is of an acceptably short duration, rotation employment is the native employment option which is most compatible with the concerns of native people for survival of their communities and of their traditional culture. In northern Canada, it typically best suits the needs of energy resource development industries as well.

Offshore Oil and the Small Community in Newfoundland

Gordon Inglis

Department of Anthropology
Memorial University of Newfoundland

NEWFOUNDLAND AND OFFSHORE PETROLEUM

The Province of Newfoundland and Labrador was poorly equipped to meet the challenge of offshore oil and gas development, for reasons rooted in her history as a fish-producing colony (Canning and Inglis, 1979). It was the rich resource of cod-fish on the Grand Banks that first attracted Europeans to Newfoundland. In the middle of the nineteenth century, she was the world's largest producer of dried salt cod, a largely self-governing entity within the British Empire in which nearly ninety percent of the male work force was employed in the fishery. By the end of the century, with an expanding population and declining markets for the staple product, the government of Newfoundland attempted to diversify the economy, following policies similar to those of Canada: a heavily-subsidized railway was built, inducements were offered to encourage agriculture and manufacturing, and attempts were made to attract international capital. Very few of the enterprises generated were successful. A steady stream of Newfoundlanders emigrated to the "Boston States" and Canada. In 1933, the economy reached such a low ebb that Newfoundland gave up independent Dominion status and was governed for sixteen years by a Commission appointed from London. Conditions improved somewhat during the Second World War with better fish markets and the building of American military bases, but when Newfoundland joined the Canadian Confederation in 1949 she was far behind the rest of the country in incomes and in services of all kinds. Massive transfers of funds from the Federal government and massive borrowing by the Provincial government greatly improved transportation, social infrastructure, and social services, but parallel efforts to secure economic development were not notably successful. In 1972, a report by the Canadian Council on Rural Development suggested that the solution to Newfoundland's chronic problems lay in the staged movement of half her population to other areas of Canada (Copes, 1972).

The history of the province is the history of a resource community writ large and Newfoundland's problems have been remarkably like those of a single-industry town. Newfoundland has been particularly vulnerable to some of the less-desirable consequences of large-scale development. It lacked a diversified industrial base and long-term development policy, and had weak municipal governments, an absence of regional government, high unemployment rates, an extremely high level of public debt, regional and local rivalry for development, dependency at all levels of the society, and uncertainty about jurisdiction over the resource and its development (Canning and Inglis, 1979).

In the five years since we made that assessment there have been many changes, but most of these basic conditions remain. The economy continues to be narrowly based on resource extraction industries of mining, forestry, and fishing. The fishery, the province's traditional mainstay, is cyclic. In 1977, with the recent acquisition of extended offshore jurisdiction, it was on an upswing, and succeeding years saw heavy capital investment by fish companies, government, and fishermen. Now the fishery is again in severe difficulty. The report of a Federal task force this autumn is likely to result in retrenchment and a narrowing of employment opportunity in that sector. Projections suggest little potential for expansion in other resource sectors (ECC, 1980).

Unemployment remains high (17%) and the rate of participation in the work force is low. Other methods of counting that allow for the "discouraged worker" phenomenon would place the number much higher (Newfoundland and Labrador Federation of Labour, 1978). In addition, over 80,000 Newfoundlanders have gone to other parts of Canada in search of work (ECC, 1980:135), many of them to Alberta. The cancellation of large development projects in the west is likely to send many of them home again, and any large-scale development in Newfoundland will almost certainly attract more.

The level of *per capita* public debt also remains the highest in the country, and in order to maintain services the Provincial government continues to borrow heavily–the current budget projects borrowing of 300 million for this year. In short, the society remains highly dependent and highly vulnerable, leaning heavily upon the Federal government for transfer payments, development assistance, make-work programmes, and other income-support programmes. Inflation and high interest rates have taken a heavy toll of local business, and Federal retrenchment in areas such as Unemployment Insurance will add to the Provincial burden.

The major changes since 1977 have been in the realm of public policy. The man who was then the relatively new and untried Minister of Mines and Energy has become Premier, and the suggestions for regulating petroleum development that were then being generated by a small group within his department form part of an overall strategy that may be characterized as an attempt to capture or re-capture provincial control over resources and their management, and to increase the amount of money accruing to the province from their exploitation. The strategy is evident in attempts to secure a greater share of the economic rent from Labrador hydro-electric power, to gain the right to transmit power across Quebec for sale in the United States, to gain control of northern cod stocks, to renegotiate forest management and royalties with pulp and paper companies, and other such efforts. Several of these disputes– including most notably the disagreement with the Federal government concerning jurisdiction over off-shore oil and gas–remain unresolved.

In the matter of offshore petroleum resources, the province has been proceeding as though it had secured jurisdiction. In an Act Respecting Petroleum and Natural Gas (Newfoundland, 1977) and accompanying guidelines (Newfoundland, 1978; 1981a) the government has attempted to ensure that:

1. a major share of the economic rent from development of the resource goes to the provincial government;
2. local businesses will be given preference in supplying and servicing for offshore exploration and production;
3. the province will participate in development of the resource through a government-owned corporation;
4. Newfoundlanders will be given preference for oil-related jobs;
5. companies engaged in petroleum development provide training for jobs for which Newfoundlanders are not now qualified;
6. petroleum companies devote a portion of annual expenditure to locally-based research and development;

7. development plans be subjected to a process of review by public hearing; and

8. the pace and sequencing of development be controlled to minimize negative impact and maximize benefits.

In addition, the government has created an administrative structure to coordinate activities relating to petroleum development. The Petroleum Directorate, a special agency under the Minister of Mines and Energy, monitors all activities related to petroleum development, and has responsibility for administering government regulations. The Offshore Petroleum Impact Committee is responsible for coordinating the work of other government departments in relation to petroleum development. It is chaired by the Clerk of the Executive Council, and is advised by five sub-committees, covering the areas of fisheries and environment, education and training, development planning, financial impact, and social and cultural impact. Four sub-committees are chaired by deputy ministers of regular government departments and each is advised by a Council of private citizens.

Thus far, all petroleum industry activity in the area has been exploratory. Since 1966, eighty-four wells have been drilled and five rigs will be drilling this season. Four discoveries of gas/condensate have been made off the Labrador coast, and one major oil discovery on the Grand Banks. In addition, there are known occurrences of gas and oil on shore in the western part of the island, where sporadic drilling activity has taken place since the 1960's (Newfoundland, 1981b). Estimates of the offshore resource recoverable over a twenty-year period range from a conservative level of 1.5 billion barrels of oil and 20 trillion cubic feet of gas to the possibility of quantities equal to or greater than the resources of the North Sea.

Considering the large areas concerned, oil and gas development in Newfoundland is still in the early exploratory phase. In anticipation of impacts, the Provincial government and other agencies have drawn heavily upon experiences in Scotland and Norway. However, forecasting has been complicated by the federal-provincial dispute over jurisdiction, changes in international markets and the fate of other Canadian energy developments. Production technology has not yet been announced. There are indications that semi-submersible rigs may be employed, in which case they are likely to be built elsewhere than in Newfoundland (Newfoundland, 1981d:8), but some possibility remains for the construction of steel or concrete platforms in the province. There is even greater uncertainty about the disposition of the oil and gas once it is brought to the surface. No firm commitments have been made to indicate whether this would involve pipelines and landfall sites, processing at the now-idle Come-by-Chance refinery owned by Petro-Canada, or removal to ships at the well-head for processing elsewhere.

After the Hibernia discovery in 1979, it was generally anticipated that development would take place more quickly than has actually occurred. It was expected that Mobil Oil would begin development for production from the Hibernia field in 1982, with actual production by 1987. In addition, it was projected that there would be increased exploration activity over the next ten years, and the phasing in of new fields for production.

The Hibernia discovery led to a flurry of speculation in real estate and business activity. In an attempt to minimize speculation and narrow the range of anticipation about development sites, the provincial government placed a partial freeze on land in nineteen areas designated as potential locations for onshore activity. Within these regulations, corporations and consortiums purchased or took options on land in some of these for servicing centres or rig-fabrication sites.

Other regulations require that petroleum operators give first preference in the provision of goods, services, and research and development to companies in which at least 51 percent of the shares are held by persons normally resident in the province. This led to a number of joint ventures between local business people and outside capital. Between the autumn of 1979 and the spring of 1981, about ninety new businesses were incorporated which were primarily concerned with oil exploration (Newfoundland, 1981c:36). Many of these were consulting companies supplying engineering and other technical services. Most of the effect of this activity was felt in St. John's, where there was a minor boom in real estate.

As I have noted, the pace of development has not been as rapid as anticipated. Mobil Oil was scheduled to present a development plan and environmental impact study for Hibernia late last year or early this year, but has now postponed it indefinitely. Production from the Hibernia field now seems unlikely to take place before 1990, if then. The pace of exploratory drilling has declined somewhat, and the tragic loss of the Ocean Ranger has added to uncertainty. None of the projected onshore site developments has taken place. In St. John's the real estate market has declined, the housing vacancy rate has climbed from near zero in late 1981 to about eight percent in May of 1982, and the number of real estate agents has dropped by about a third. In the same period, some 70 businesses in St. John's have closed, moved, or gone bankrupt (*Daily News* May 20, 1982:15).

Thus far, apart from this cycle of speculation, probably the major economic impact of exploration has been in income to local residents from jobs in offshore drilling and servicing (Newfoundland, 1981c:44). In each of the past two years, about a thousand Newfoundlanders have been employed directly in these activities, though not necessarily for the full year. Most projections (Newfoundland, 1981c; ECC, 1980) indicate that even if the pace of development should accelerate, the total number of such jobs to be expected is not great. According to the Economic Council of Canada (1980:128,146), only rapid development on the scale of the North Sea would have any substantial impact on the rate of unemployment, and most jobs created in this way would not be permanent. Nonetheless, because of high rates of unemployment, oil-related jobs are a major theme of expectation, especially in small communities, and oil-generated employment is a central political issue.

IMPLICATIONS FOR COMMUNITY DEVELOPMENT

If Newfoundland as a province is structurally vulnerable to detrimental effects from large oil development, her small and rural communities are even more so. Lack of industrial base, capital, and managerial skills means that there will be little possibility for small communities to take advantage of business opportunities. High unemployment and under-employment may lead to uncritical acceptance of development regardless of social cost. Weak municipal governments and the lack of regional government may put rural areas at a disadvantage in dealing with developers.

On the other hand, a number of structures and agencies exist to provide support to rural communities in dealing with development. In the rural areas themselves, besides municipal governments, there are Regional Development Associations, service clubs, fishermen's committees, branches of the union that includes fishermen and fish plant workers, and other voluntary groups. Within the Provincial government the Petroleum Directorate includes on its staff a community liaison officer responsible for contact with community groups, a sociologist responsible for research in the field, and other specialists. The Offshore Petroleum Impact Group has a sub-committee on social and cultural impact. Other government departments, such as Social Services, Culture Recreation and Youth, Education, Health, Labour, and so on, which deal with communities in their own fields, include petroleum development in their purview. For one example, the Department of Rural, Agricultural, and Northern Development provides services and incentives in business and crafts development for rural areas, and has undertaken research and planning for the application of these programmes to oil-related developments (DRAND, 1980).

The Memorial University Extension Services, which has field workers in several areas, has produced a body of film, video-tape, and print material on petroleum development, and carries out community information seminars on various aspects of development impact. Other agencies include various church groups, an Inter-Church Committee, the Community Services Council, the Rural Development Council, the Association for Adult Education and similar community-oriented organizations. Mobil Oil, through its local public relations section, has also provided information sessions for community groups. All of these agencies draw upon a large body of information from the Scottish and Norwegian experiences with North Sea development.

AREAS OF POTENTIAL DIRECT IMPACT

Persons involved in the support organizations have identified four or five areas outside of St. John's as most likely to experience direct effects from development. These areas differ widely from one another in present characteristics, in the nature of anticipated effects, and in the likelihood of development.

The Southern Shore is a string of small communities along the coastline for about 140 kilometers from St. John's. The fishery is important in most of them, and a number of residents commute to work in the city. The area may expect some spin-off activity from St. John's, and would be among the first to suffer from the effects of oil spills at the Hibernia field.

An impact committee has been in existence on the Southern Shore for about two years. This committee has worked with the community liaison officer of the Petroleum Directorate, and has solicited information from Mobil Oil and the University Extension Service. It involves a cross-section of the communities, but a major impetus has come from local officials of the Department of Social Services. The committee has identified its main concerns as local government, education, fisheries, lifestyle and culture and has set up sub-committees on each.

When the provincial government circulated its proposed guidelines for development of the Hibernia field, this committee offered a number of recommendations, some of which were incorporated in the final guidelines document. The Petroleum Directorate regards the committee as something of a prototype, and representatives of it have travelled to other communities and other provinces to talk about their experiences.

The second area, Bay Roberts, is a local service centre embedded in a strip of fairly dense rural population along the northwestern shore of Conception Bay. It is not a fishing centre, but the fishery is important in

several neighbouring communities. A development company has purchased land in Bay Roberts in anticipation of harbour development for
offshore servicing.

A rather loosely-organized local committee has been working with
the University Extension Service field worker and a representative of the
United Church. There has also been involvement by local officials of the
provincial Department of Social Services. Concerns centre around business opportunities, impact on local real estate, jobs, and social impacts.

The third area, Placentia, is a marine transportation terminus for the
South Coast. At one time there was consideration of the possibility of
using facilities belonging to the once very large U.S. naval base at Ar-
gentia for offshore service development. A development committee was
formed there with the assistance of the Social Action Committee of the
Roman Catholic Archdiocese. This committee has been less business-
oriented than, for example, the Bay Roberts group, and has remained
aloof from a local Rural Development Association and the provincial
Rural Development Council.

Recently expectation of offshore oil-related development in this area
has receded, and the committee has turned its attention to larger development issues such as Federal cuts in marine transportation services in
Placentia Bay.

Finally, Marystown is the most industrialized of the areas under
consideration, having a shipyard and a fish processing plant. A development consortium took options on nearby land in a deep-water bay for
possible development of a rig-fabrication site. Interest has been high
among business people and municipal authorities, but relatively little
involvement by citizen groups is reported.

Interest and involvement were high immediately after the Hibernia
discovery in the spring of 1979, and remained so until about the autumn
of 1981. Continued uncertainty about the course of development and a
lack of visible activity has resulted in a decline of interest since then. The
Memorial University Extension Service, for example, report that they
have carried out 250 to 300 community information seminars in the past
three years, but that in the past six to eight months there has been very
little demand for this service.

When local interest was at its height, business people were interested
in economic advantages, fishermen in pollution and environmental effects, and municipal governments in effects on population and local
services. Concern about possible negative social impact came largely
from church groups, teachers, and workers with the Department of Social
Services. Partly in response to this variety, the University Extension
Service has developed information modules oriented to various specialized interests.

Representatives of several of the support agencies express the opinion that in many rural areas the desire for jobs and economic benefits has been sufficiently strong to mute discussion of possible negative social impact. They feel that there has been some tendency for persons expressing such concerns to be labelled "anti-development" and charged with endangering the area's chances to reap benefits. This suggests a potential for intra-community conflict when development possibilities move nearer to realization.

Workers also report that in spite of the efforts of support agencies and local committees, misconceptions about the nature of potential development are still pervasive. Expectations about the numbers of jobs and the level of activity tend to be vastly inflated. Many people still expect the impact to come from large-scale activities by oil companies themselves rather than from smaller operations by contracting and sub-contracting firms.

Some of the people involved feel that the present period of delay could be advantageous to community groups, giving them time to reflect and prepare for eventual impact. However, they feel that this will not happen without a stronger active programme by provincial government authorities. Although most of the agencies have exerted some effort to stimulate community involvement, the overall approach has been to support rather than initiate community action. Some workers feel that in spite of official government statements about concern for the protection of rural society and ways of life, social and cultural impact has received less attention than it should. They point out that the Advisory Council on social and cultural impact of the governments' Offshore Petroleum Impact Committee was the last to be formed, and has been without a chairman and has not met since July of 1981.

The main problem now faced by interested persons in the small communities and workers with the support agencies is that of maintaining public interest and participation in the absence of visible activity or even of concrete development proposals. Some workers express concern that in these circumstances efforts to stimulate interest may be misguided: they argue that if a high level of public involvement is generated and the delays continue, people may be come disillusioned and apathetic, and less willing to become involved when development is closer. Others argue that a broad-based community-development programme, not specifically tied to oil development, should be instituted now with the intention of strengthening existing local structures and creating others that will be capable of a quick response when development becomes imminent. They point out that, in fact, the trend has been in the opposite direction, with a reduction in community development activity by such agencies as the University Extension Service.

With the support of the local office of the Department of the Secretary of State, several of the support agencies have formed a Resource Development Impact Group and initiated a project which will compile bibliographic and information resources and draw up a plan for community involvement. This will prepare for the public hearing process required by both federal and provincial government regulations before actual development begins. It is intended that the plan be operated as a pilot project in one area, modified in the light of that process, and then carried to other areas.

AREAS OF POTENTIAL INDIRECT IMPACT

The majority of Newfoundland's rural communities and settlements will not experience direct impact. Originally, the large number of small settlements dotted around Newfoundland's coastline came into being as places from which to pursue a small-boat fishery (Inglis, 1980). Until the 1950s, fishermen and their families maintained themselves by a seasonal round that could include the inshore and Labrador or Banks fisheries, sealing, small-scale agriculture, hunting, small stock-keeping, wood-cutting, and house and boat building. With modernization, some of the more isolated settlements have been abandoned, but there are still over eight hundred such communities, about half of them with populations of fewer than five hundred. Their people may still achieve part of their maintenance from the activities mentioned above (or their modern variants) and from such new sources as wage work in construction or fish processing, periods of employment in other places, commuting to employment, make-work projects, Unemployment Insurance, and Social Assistance.

Whereas these small communities were at one time separate and largely self-sufficient, linked separately and independently to a few major service centres and to overseas markets, they are now interlinked into a complex network by roads and communication networks. In a given family, the younger children may go to school in one community, older children in another, the woman of the house may have periods of employment at a fish plant in a third, and the man may commute to work in a larger centre. With the exception of a few places on the South Coast and in Labrador, most rural residents are within driving distance of service centres with urban-style amenities for shopping and entertainment. One of the factors that makes the rural lifestyle attractive is housing. Land is still cheap, and many rural families can make free building sites available. Land taxes are minimal or non-existent. It is still possible for a man to cut and haul his own timber, and have it sawn cheaply at a small push-bench sawmill. Periods of Unemployment Insurance or Social Assistance allow time for building and kin-networks provide additional labour. As a consequence, many rural residents can have good housing at low cost. For many men, a stable family base in good housing near the support of kin and friends make it possible to take advantage of short term, highly paid employment away from home.

Large scale developments in a few centres would be unlikely to have much direct effect on this basic adaptation. Many rural residents would undoubtedly wish to take advantage of employment opportunities, but it seems likely that this could be incorporated into the existing patterns. Given the high rates of rural unemployment and under employment, it seems unlikely that there would be any major impact on the fishery from competition for labour.

However, a number of existing trends in the society already seem to have the potential for pronounced effects upon the rural adaptation. For example, there is a growing trend toward the organization of municipal governments, and pressure to cause them to raise some of their own revenue. The widespread imposition of land taxes could make profound changes in the pattern of rural land-holding and housing. Inflation and higher transport costs could reduce the range within which rural people can pursue employment, shopping, or entertainment. The centralization and mechanization of the fishery would remove a source of seasonal work and income for some rural people. Tightening of Unemployment Insurance regulations will make seasonal work patterns less remunerative. If oil development were to accelerate such trends without providing increased opportunity for generating household income in the rural areas, its effects on small communities could be profound.

SOME CONCLUSIONS

The Province of Newfoundland and her rural communities suffer from certain disadvantages in the face of large-scale oil development. It may be, in fact, that the major impact of offshore oil so far has been the formulation of a public resolve to use the development to gain a greater degree of economic independence for the province, and a greater control over her future.

If development proceeds, and especially if production rigs should be built in Newfoundland, some small communities may experience very heavy impacts, comparable to that of major construction projects such as hydroelectric dams. Most small communities, however, may expect to experience only indirect effects. Experience in Scotland (McNicoll, 1982) suggests that oil industry development by itself has provided relatively little stimulus to local income or employment in rural areas. The primary opportunity for rural residents will be in the availability of limited-term construction jobs, a familiar pattern to many rural Newfoundlanders, who have traditionally taken advantage of such opportunities in other parts of the province and elsewhere in Canada. Given high rates of unemployment and the nature of the fishing industry, there is little reason to expect a major impact on employment in the fishery (DRAND, 1980; NORDCO, 1982). Oil spills or interference with fishing patterns, of course, could create other sorts of problems. There is a reasonably strong and well-informed network of support services available to assist smaller communities in anticipating and dealing with oil development impact, but the system seems to suffer from a lack of coordination and strong leadership, and there is reason to fear that it could not respond quickly enough should development suddenly accelerate. A concerted, broad-based community development programme, not directly tied to oil development, would be a desirable next step.

Even with the best of community development programmes, the fundamental problems of Newfoundland will remain those of a large-scale resource community, and petroleum development may provide only a temporary alleviation. If the provincial government's attempts to acquire a greater share of economic benefits are successful, the effect would be to reduce–or even eliminate–the province's dependence upon Federal transfers, but this, by itself, would not change the basic situation. It would appear that a truly constructive community development programme for Newfoundland in the petroleum era would be one that incorporates a plan for translating the financial gains into expansion and diversification of the economic base. Thus far, none of the agencies involved has demonstrated the ability to generate or promote such a plan.

A Systems Approach to Impact Management:

Program Design and Implementation Considerations

F. Larry Leistritz
Department of Agricultural Economics
North Dakota State University

John M. Halstead
Department of Agricultural Economics
North Dakota State University

Robert A. Chase
Department of Agricultural Economics
North Dakota State University

Steve H. Murdock
Department of Rural Sociology
Texas A&M University

INTRODUCTION

The economic and social effects of large-scale development projects have received increased attention by both researchers and decision makers in recent years. Since the mid-1970s, a growing number of analyses and case studies have been published, providing ever-expanding insights concerning the effects of such projects on nearby communities (Gilmore and Duff 1975; Summers et al. 1976; Albrecht 1978; Summers and Selvik 1979; Murdock and Leistritz 1979).

Despite a growing awareness of the importance of socioeconomic impacts, the processes for coping with project effects have received limited attention in the literature. Whereas the nature of and methods for predicting socioeconomic changes stemming from energy resource projects have been the subject of considerable analysis (Albrecht, 1978;

137

Gilmore et al., 1976; Mountain West Research, Inc. 1975; Denver Research Institute 1979; Leistritz and Murdock 1981) mechanisms to mitigate the socioeconomic effects of a project on nearby communities have received only a cursory treatment. Those reviews of "impact mitigation" which have appeared typically discuss only a few selected impact management measures (Metz 1982; Metz 1981; Myhra, 1980), or they review only a few selected cases where developers or communities have taken an active role in influencing project outcomes (Peelle 1979; Gilmore et al. 1981; Leistritz and Maki 1981; Metz, 1980). Also they fail to consider the cumulative and interactive effects of multiple impact management measures and provide little basis for evaluating alternative approaches or the conditions under which each may be most effective.

Perhaps the major weakness of such attempts is their failure to develop an adequate conceptual basis for viewing and managing impact events. Impacts occur within a set of interrelated systems: local, regional and even national systems affect such impacts. Thus, if impacts are to be understood and effectively managed, they must be seen as occurring within a set of interdependent systems; therefore, economic and social systems theory can be used to increase our understanding of the essential elements of an impact management system.

Existing system theories reveal that exogenous events, such as the impacts of major resource developers, are likely to disturb the basic equilibrium of the local and regional socioeconomic systems (Parsons 1951; Buckley 1967). They indicate the need to view impact management in terms of both its local and national implications. Systems theory also suggests that the key to understanding and managing a system lies in seeing such systems as an integrated complex in which the inputs, internal relationships and outputs must be assessed and measured. The need to integrate the impact management process and to use a comprehensive approach which measures expected impacts (the impact assessment process), their effects on system elements (impact management), and system outputs (through monitoring programs) is made clear through the use of a systems approach. In addition, such an approach suggests that impact mitigation can best be effected by altering the magnitude of the exogenous variables (the impacts), by strengthening selected parts of the system (enhancing local capabilities), and by initiating programs to retain or restore the equilibrium of the system (compensation and incentives). Finally, the use of such an approach suggests a need to implement the processes of identifying the system of interest, its essential elements and the interrelationships among them throughout the impact management process.

A systems approach thus appears to be applicable to the impact management process. Although it cannot provide specific guidelines for impact management, it offers a valuable perspective for ensuring that impact management activities are seen in an integrated and inclusive manner.

This paper attempts to address impact management from a systems perspective. First, the interrelated nature of impact events that clarify the need for an integrated socioeconomic impact management framework is discussed. Second,the key components of such a management system are presented. Third, the implementation of an impact management program within a systems context is discussed, with emphasis on the relationship between impact management activities and project development (system) phases. Finally, conclusions are presented and implications for future research are discussed.

THE IMPACT MANAGEMENT FRAMEWORK

While impact mitigation has been discussed more frequently in recent years, precedents for these activities go back several decades. Notable among the early examples of impact mitigation activities were the efforts of various resource developers to establish housing and support services (i.e. "company towns") for their workers. Construction of self-contained communities was common in mining and forestry from 1850 to 1950 and still occurs in remote areas (Metz 1979).

The term "impact mitigation" came into widespread usage following its inclusion in NEPA. There has been a common tendency, however, to view impact mitigation in a narrow context of merely "reducing or eliminating negative impacts" (O'Hare *et al.* 1982; Urban Systems, Inc. 1980). Likewise, developers' efforts at impact mitigation have often been narrow and reactive. Such efforts typically have focussed on only a few key impact dimensions, have failed to consider the full range of options which might be available and have been initiated only after problems became apparent (Metz 1979; Myhra 1980; Faas 1982; Halstead *et al.* 1982).

In formulating appropriate responses to the potential socioeconomic effects of large-scale development projects sited in rural areas, the concept of "impact mitigation" described above appears too narrow. A broader and more comprehensive approach, encompassing measures which enhance the project's local benefits and which provides for various forms of compensation to local interests, as well as actions to reduce or eliminate negative effects, is needed. Hence, we, and others (Gilmore *et al.* 1981; Berkey *et al.* 1977) believe that the term "impact management" is more appropriate.

The objectives of an impact management program are to anticipate and alleviate undesirable project effects *and* to enhance effects which are deemed beneficial. The use of a systems perspective in impact management stresses the need for an integrated approach involving four elements: (1) the need for a comprehensive approach; (2) the need to integrate the impact management activities with the overall project development schedule; (3) the need to involve all key interests and groups; and (4) the need to deal realistically with the uncertainties inherent in the development process.

In designing an impact management program, it is important that the full range of project management and community growth management options that may be relevant be considered. It is also important to consider potential interactions of various management measures and to evaluate trade-offs between alternatives.

The integration of impact management considerations into the overall project planning and development process requires adequate lead time. It is thus desirable for a preliminary impact evaluation/issue identification to occur during the feasibility analysis of the project. An evaluation early in the project planning process permits scoping future impact assessment and management activities, allows adequate time for management efforts to be incorporated into the project schedule, and enables explicit incorporation of impact management costs into the project budget (Luke 1980). As project planning proceeds, it is essential to provide appropriate lead time for the completion of a detailed impact assessment and community growth management plans. Subsequently, additional time will be required to design, finance and construct facilities by the time they will be needed.

A third major consideration in impact management is the need to involve all key actors. An approach which has proven to be effective in the western U.S. has been the formation of impact management teams. These bodies have typically included representatives of a range of local interests and, in some cases, state and federal agencies. They have reviewed impact assessments and mitigation plans and have often been able to reach an effective concensus concerning acceptable impact management procedures (Myhra 1980).

A final consideration in designing an impact management program is the need to deal with the uncertainties inherent in the development process. Uncertainty concerning both the future of the project and the magnitude and distribution of its socioeconomic effects invariably complicates impact management (Gilmore et al. 1981). Such uncertainty cannot be entirely eliminated. It is therefore essential that the impact management plant be sufficiently flexible to allow for modification and that a system for monitoring both project impacts and the effectiveness of management responses be incorporated into the overall framework (Leistritz and Chase 1982; DePape 1982).

IMPACT MANAGEMENT-A SYSTEMS FRAMEWORK

An overall impact management system requires the measurement and management of system inputs, interrelationships and outputs. This approach suggests the need to focus on three basic elements: (1) an Impact Assessment System; (2) an Impact Management Plan; and (3) and Impact Monitoring System. A simplified schematic diagram illustrating the major dimensions of each component and their interrelationships is presented in Figure 1.

Impact Assessment System

The purpose of the impact assessment system is to forecast project-induced changes in various social and economic variables in order to anticipate potential problem areas where impact management efforts will be needed. It is also useful in identifying opportunities for enhancement of project-related benefits. The impact assessment system thus plays a primary role in guiding impact management efforts.

The basic impact assessment procedure uses as inputs key characteristics of the development project (e.g., work force, taxable value of facilities) and of the site area (e.g., economic base, population composition). Appropriate economic, demographic, and social assessment techniques are then employed to forecast the various effects of project development and resulting changes in public sector demands, costs and revenues and various social factors. The demands on local economic, governmental, and social systems are then compared with the capacity or response capability of such systems. Areas where the potential for shortfalls and related problems is substantial are identified as requiring management attention (see Figure 1).

Because impact assessment methods have been described in detail elsewhere (Leistritz and Murdock 1981), they are not discussed in depth here. Two factors, however, are of overriding importance in designing and implementing an impact assessment system. First, it is imperative that the system be oriented to the needs of decision makers–the clientele of the assessment effort. It must address the policy makers' major concerns and must provide projections for appropriate time periods (usually annual) and for the jurisdictional levels at which key decisions are made.

A second major design consideration relates to the need for realistically addressing the uncertainties inherent in the impact process. The system should allow for easy alteration of key parameters (e.g., project scheduling, work force levels, etc.) and thus facilitate the presentation of impact projections in terms of multiple scenarios and ranges of impacts. It should also allow for updating of projections in light of changing

Figure 1. Major Components of an Impact Management System

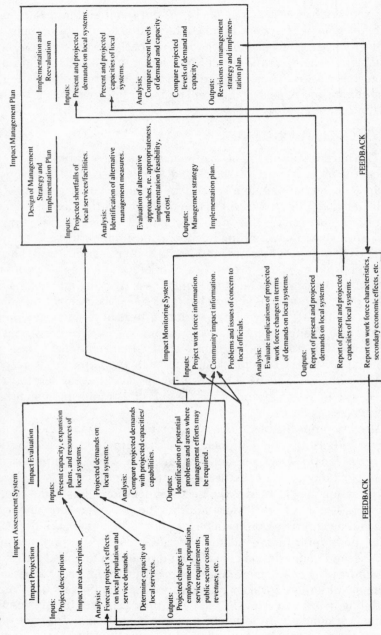

conditions. Finally, if several projects are being developed in the same areas, the assessment system should allow for evaluation of cumulative, as well as project-specific, impacts.

Impact Management Plan

The impact management plan presents the set of actions which will be taken to minimize the costs and maximize the benefits presented by the project to local residents, to compensate individuals or groups adversely affected by the project, and/or to provide incentives for community acceptance of the facility. A systems perspective suggests that impact management could be affected by altering the exogenous factors affecting the system, the elements of the system, or by measures to restore equilibrium. The types of measures which may be included in an impact management plan thus typically fall into three general categories: (1) measures to minimize demands on local systems (economic, governmental, and social); (2) measures to enhance the capacity of local systems to cope with change; and (3) measures to compensate individuals or groups. The extent to which these various actions may be applicable to a specific project will depend mainly on the nature and location of the project and the institutional setting within which it occurs.

Minimizing Demands on Local Systems

Local socioeconomic impacts of resource development projects are associated with the inmigration of project workers and their families to the site area. Measures to lessen demands on local systems tend to focus on reducing the number of relocating workers and dependents. Approaches to achieving this goal fall into two general categories: (1) alterations in facility design or construction schedule; and (2) work force policies geared to reducing the proportion of workers which will migrate to the site area (Table 1).

There are three major alterations in facility design or construction schedule which could reduce the demands imposed on the site area: (1) lengthening the project construction period; (2) fabricating some facility components at off-site locations; and (3) staggering unit construction schedules for multiple-unit facilities (see Table 1). The economic forces and geological imperatives which affect the siting and development of resource projects, however, seem to limit the applicability of these measures in many cases.

Given the project site and construction parameters, the principal method for lessening local impacts is to reduce the proportion of inmigrating workers. This strategy has two major options. The first is to increase the number of local workers hired through local hiring preference and/or training programs. Increased local hiring will reduce migration

Measures to Reduce Inmigration

OPTION	METHOD	ADVANTAGES	DISADVANTAGES/ LIMITATIONS
1) Alterations in facility design for construction schedule	1) Lengthening construction period	– reduces peak work force requirements – reduces number of relocating workers	– increases project cost
	2) Off-site component fabrication	– increases construction efficiency – eases needs for craftsmen and engineers on-site	– may be limited by union-employer contractual agreements and/or capability to transport large components
	3) Scheduling of multiple units	– reduces peak work force requirements	– is applicable only to projects with multiple units or when several projects are planned for the same area
2) Reducing the percentage of inmigrating project workers and families	1) Increasing local hiring a) local hiring preference	– increases percentage of economic benefits accruing to local residents – enhances stability of work force	– may violate union-labor agreements – may be viewed as discriminatory – increases competition for local labor with area businesses – success depends on current employment situation in area
	b) training programs	– may reduce projects' competition with local employers – is popular with local residents – increases number of workers hired locally	– may not increase local hiring due to union-labor contractual agreements – requires careful initiation, lead-time consideration

Measures to Reduce Inmigration

OPTION	METHOD	ADVANTAGES	DISADVANTAGES/ LIMITATIONS
	2) Increasing commuting a) measures to reduce travel costs b) provision of temporary housing	– increases ease of labor force recruitment – increases productivity – reduces number of relocating workers	– may aggravate local traffic problems – induces payroll leakages from local community – may lead to higher turnover

into the area and will also enhance local economic benefits, thereby increasing community acceptance of the project. Local hiring may be limited, however, by a number of factors (Table 1).

The second major alternative involves measures to encourage commuting. These attempt to reduce workers' travel costs or provide convenient accommodations for those who commute weekly. Measures to reduce workers' travel costs may include direct provision of transportation or provision of travel allowances. Temporary housing could be provided on-site. This may encourage workers to commute on a weekly basis.

Increasing commuting may generate additional problems, however. First, traffic problems on local roads may be aggravated. An increase in multiple ridership, perhaps through increased use of buses and vans, is a means of alleviating this problem. Second, increased commuting may be seen by locals as causing project benefits to leave the area. Finally, high levels of commuting may lead to higher worker turnover rates.

Enhancing the Capacity of Local Systems

Even though the level of inmigration associated with project development may be reduced, a large-scale facility will generate significant population growth and increases in the demands on local systems. It is necessary, therefore, to consider impact management measures which enhance the capability of local systems to cope with change. The literature suggests that such measures fall into five general categories: (1) local planning assistance; (2) provision by the developer of housing and infrastructure; (3) financial assistance to the local public sector, particularly front-end financing; (4) stimulation of housing development and business expansion by the local private sector; and (5) enhancement of local protection capabilities (Aronson 1981; Briscoe, Maphis, Murray, and Lamont, Inc. 1978; Faas 1982; Metz 1980; Myhra 1980).

One of the most important activities in developing an impact management program is initiating advanced planning at the local level. This is a common problem for small communities, which seldom have the capabilities to manage rapid growth (Greene and Curry 1977). The local planning phase of the growth impact management task is of greatest value during the predevelopment stage, and should begin as soon as the community learns of the project. Timing is important, since more planning lead time given to the community generally results in more successful mitigation efforts. The developer can facilitate these planning efforts by providing technical assistance and funding.

The most obvious problem encountered by impacted communities is inadequate housing for the new population. The relocation of a large portion of the project work force will increase area housing demand. In the absence of adequate planning, this increase may result in inflated housing prices, rental fees, property values, and property taxes.

Since it is in the best interest of the developer to assure an adequate supply of housing near the project, measures may be taken to increase the housing stock. These include construction of a self-contained community, development of permanent housing or mobile home parks, revitalization of existing housing, or provision of temporary housing. While energy development firms have frequently provided housing and related infrastructure, most efforts by developers have been aimed at stimulating private housing developers (Aronson 1981; Metz 1979).

These efforts often take the form of assembling developable land or guaranteeing purchase or occupancy of new housing units. Because uncertainty often inhibits local developers from initiating new housing construction, such guarantees will often be effective in stimulating development. Similarly, uncertainty concerning the future of the project and the magnitude of local growth may retard local business expansion. If such expansion is perceived as desirable, the resource developer can stimulate it by establishing long-term contracts for supplies or services with selected local businesses. With such contracts in hand, local businesses typically find financing for expansion much easier to obtain.

When rapid development occurs, local governments typically face a cost-revenue squeeze. Substantial capital costs often must be incurred to provide for necessary expansion of service capacity at a time well before significant development-related revenues are received. In such cases, it may be necessary for local governments to rely on grants from senior governments (which often cover only capital, not operating costs) prepayment of sales or property taxes by the developer, borrowing, or other front-end financing mechanisms.

Compensation Measures

Development of any large-scale facility will almost invariably lead to some adverse effects on local groups and communities. Compensation mechanisms are needed to redress individuals and groups who experience such effects. *Compensation* is defined as the provision of monetary payments or other benefits to local interests to compensate for project-induced costs or losses. Compensation, which seeks to make affected parties as well off as they were prior to development, can be contrasted with *incentives*, which provide benefits above and beyond the costs incurred (Urban Systems, Inc. 1980).

Compensation measures can take one of four basic forms: (1) monetary; (2) conditional; (3) in-kind; and (4) offsetting. Direct monetary payments are most frequently employed. They are used to compensate landowners whose property is taken in the course of development; likewise, direct payments are made by developers to local governments to compensate for construction phase fiscal deficits (Faas, 1982).

Conditional compensation mechanisms are implemented only if a particular adverse circumstance occurs. For example, a developer might post a surety bond or acquire liability insurance as a guarantee that facility closure and cleanup costs will be covered or to provide for compensation in case of a facility-related accident.

In-kind compensation typically involves replacement of lost amenities. For instance, a developer might dedicate lands for park and recreation purposes or contribute funds for wildlife habitat preservation to compensate for recreational opportunities or habitats foreclosed by development (O'Hare *et al.* 1982).

The offsetting compensation concept recognizes that some adverse effects of development are virtually impossible to prevent (e.g., loss of small town atmosphere) but that creation or enhancement of benefits in other areas (e.g., attractive job opportunities, improved community facilities) may in some sense offset the negative effects. This concept is being employed increasingly as an overt strategy of impact management in connection with some Canadian resource communities (DePape 1982).

An effective compensation plan involves several steps. First, impacts must be identified during the assessment phase. Second, groups entitled to receive compensation must be determined. This involves identifying those who desire compensation, assessing the validity of the claim and determining the level of compensation to be paid. Third, a method of payment must be chosen. Finally, the terms of payment must be specified.

The literature suggests that at least five types of local groups may be entitled to compensation (Halstead *et al.* 1982; Metz 1980; Myhra 1980;

Morrell and Magorian 1982; O'Hare *et al.*, 1982). These include (1) local landowners whose property is taken for facility development; (2) nearby landowners whose property may be diminished in value; (3) local governments which experience significant fiscal deficits; (4) low and fixed income groups affected by local inflationary effects; and (5) environmental groups. The precedents for compensation vary among these types of claimants and appear to be strongest for the first and third categories (Rice *et al.* 1980; Faas 1982; O'Hare *et al.* 1982). In most cases, negotiation between the developer and the affected parties will be vital in reaching a mutually agreeable settlement.

In summarizing the impact management plan, several other considerations deserve mention. First, the plan should provide measureable goals or targets against which the management effort can be evaluated. Thus, it may be useful to specify target values (by time period if relevant) for such factors as local hire rates, payment formulae and number of housing units to be developed. Second, the plan should explicitly identify the responsibilities of the major parties-at-interest. Finally, the plan should provide a mechanism for periodic review and revision in light of changing conditions and a means for resolving disputes which may arise. An ongoing review and evaluation of the management plan requires current and accurate information concerning the effects of project development and the efficacy of the impact management measures in dealing with them. This information can be provided by an impact monitoring system.

Impact Monitoring System

An impact monitoring system should provide accurate and timely socioeconomic information for decision makers involved in impact management activities (see Figure 1). Such information enables project officials and community leaders to assess community needs and revise mitigation plans and also serves as the basis for revised impact projections. Thus at any given time, the monitoring system allows the effectiveness of impact management activities to be evaluated while providing the information necessary for future mitigation efforts. This iterative process should continue throughout the project development period.

In response to the need for timely and accurate information, several monitoring systems have been implemented which review economic and social changes as they occur. These systems differ substantially in a number of important respects: for example, in the indicators evaluated, the mechanisms for and the frequency of data collection and the frequency of reporting (Leistritz and Chase 1982). In designing such a system, two considerations are especially important. First, the primary purpose of the system is to supply current information for impact management decisions. The types of data collected should be closely linked to expected impacts and priority issues. While selectivity is a key consideration, however, the system must be sufficiently comprehensive to achieve its purposes. Trade-offs are required to choose variables to be included as well in determining the frequency of monitoring and the number of communities to be included.

Second, the capability to utilize monitored information to develop updated impact projections is essential. The system should be designed to rapidly detect departures of key impact parameters (e.g., project schedules) from assumed levels and to reflect these changes in revised projections. Thus impact assessment techniques are not merely mechanisms for developing onetime anticipatory projections; they are impact management tools to be used through the project development.

PROGRAM IMPLEMENTATION

Implementing a successful impact management program can be a very complex undertaking and the task deserves concerted attention by the developer. In order to ensure that impact management efforts do receive continuing attention, an individual or group within the developer's organization should be assigned specific responsibility for implementing the impact management program (Luke 1980).

Management of socioeconomic impacts should be a major concern in predevelopment planning. Impact management efforts should thus be integrated with engineering and regulatory schedules in the developer's critical path charts and budgets. A schedule of major impact management activities relative to the states of project development is presented in Table 2. During initial project planning, it is important to estimate the cost of impact management efforts and to include these in the project's capital budget.

In order to develop an initial estimate of the nature, magnitude, and cost of impact management activities, a preliminary issue identification/ impact evaluation should be conducted early in the project planning period. This analysis identifies potential risks and costs, as well as benefits, to local interests and brings these factors to the attention of project managment at the project feasibility study stage. This preliminary analysis should include an evaluation of the regulatory environment and a review of the political climate.

In dealing with local interests, the developer must establish an open decision process by involving concerned local groups early in the planning process. Information, even though it is only preliminary, should be provided in as open and timely a fashion as possible and efforts should be made to develop an atmosphere of trust with local representatives (Luke 1980). Once a site has been selected for detailed evaluation, a more structured framework for interacting with various local interests may be desirable. As noted earlier, impact committees are an effective means of organizing local input. A grant from the developer may be needed to finance the activities of such a group (Myhra 1980).

Table 2.

CHRONOLOGICAL SEQUENCE OF KEY IMPACT
MANAGEMENT ACTIVITIES.

Project Phase	Impact Management
Feasibility Analysis and Site Selection	Preliminary reconnaissance level impact evaluation/issue identification Public involvement at macro level Information dissemination
Site Evaluation and Permitting	Formation of local impact committee (planning grant) Conduct anticipatory impact assessment Prepare impact management plan
Post-Permit Preparations	Obtain final funding commitments More detailed design of mitigation measures Initiate implementation of selected measures (training programs, housing and infrastructure development) Initiate monitoring of community indicators
Construction	Complete implementation of impact management plan (with periodic evaluation) Complete implementation of monitoring system (with periodic reassessments) Coordinated information exchange with public
Operation	Implementation of impact management plan continues with shift to measures to accommodate more permanent population Continue monitoring Ongoing public participation
Closure	Interaction with community re economic readjustment (perhaps via Impact Committee) Monitoring for several years following closure to assure successful economic readjustment

One of the first major tasks of the impact management committee should be to assist in scoping the anticipatory impact assessment. The committee, as well as representatives of relevant government units and regulatory bodies, should be able to review and approve the study plan and subsequently the impact assessment report.

The impact committee should also play a major role in the development of the impact management plan. The plan should be responsive to local concerns and of high professional quality so that questions do not arise later as to its validity and objectivity. Acceptability of the final plan to both the developer and local interests can help avert conflict in negotiations and compensation agreements (Sanderson, 1979).

When a number of projects are expected to affect the same area, an interindustry group to coordinate the impact management efforts of the developers may be desirable. Determining the overall implications of various changes with multiple projects and overlapping impact areas may require information and assessment capabilities which no individual developer or jurisdiction possesses. An area Council of Governments, state agency or an inter-industry group may be an appropriate entity to provide comprehensive regional impact assessments in such cases. While the most appropriate division of responsibilities among participating parties may differ greatly across localities, a general consideration is that the responsibilities assigned to a given organization should be commensurate with its resources.

SUMMARY, CONCLUSIONS AND IMPLICATIONS

While the effective management of project effects is the end toward which all impact research and assessment efforts are directed, an integrated concept of an approach to impact management has been notably lacking. We suggest a systems framework will meet this need. The detailed design of the impact management program will differ significantly from project to project. Such variations stem largely from differences in the institutional context and in project characteristics and site area conditions, which together primarily determine the nature and magnitude of project effects and local residents' perceptions of them.

The impact management framework presented here suggests numerous areas, related to the developmental context for future research. For example, one could examine such topics as:

1) The effectiveness of various recruitment and training programs in stimulating local employment.

2) The usefulness of measures to encourage long distance commuting as an alternative to work force relocation. Worker transportation and temporary housing programs could be evaluated in terms of relative costs and their effects on worker productivity, turnover, and absenteeism as well as community attitudes and perceptions.

3) Advantages and disadvantages associated with alternative mechanisms for providing front-end financing to local governments.

In addition, the framework suggests numerous areas for research concerning institutional and policy dimensions of impact management, including:

1) Determination of the most appropriate roles for various interests to play in the management process (for example, what role can state and federal governments most usefully play?);

2) Evaluation of alternative approaches to public involvement and information dissemination; and

3) Further evaluation of the applicability of alternative models for the facility siting process (e.g., local veto power, negotiation).

Finally, greater attention should be given to the long-term implications of energy resource development and especially to the ultimate closure of energy facilities (Root 1979; Hansen et al. 1981).

Overall, then, socioeconomic impact management offers a wide array of opportunities for future research. A multi-nation comparative study offers a promising vehicle for such analysis as it affords the opportunity to examine a wider range of projects, site areas, and particularly institutional contexts.

Phasing and Timing of Projects:

Decommissioning and Shutdown Issues

Kenneth A. Root

Department of Sociology
Luther College,
Decorah, Iowa

INTRODUCTION

Dubuque, Iowa is two hours from my home. An industrial community of 62,000 residents situated on the Mississippi River, Dubuque is, by Iowa standards, a large city. But it is Dubuque's unemployment that generates news headlines. While the national unemployment rate was 8.5 % last January, Dubuque's unemployment rate was one of the nation's highest, reaching 23%. According to *The Wall Street Journal*:

> That figure was inflated by a temporary shutdown at one big plant, but the rate remained a high 14.5 percent in March and will leap again in October when Dubuque Packing Co. closes its plant for good, dismissing 1,200 more workers (Gigot, 1982).

A recent *Des Moines Register* carried a front page story on the "Children of the Unemployed" (Ricchiardi, 1982), describing displaced Dubuque worker families with less money at home and some high schoolers not able to attend the high school prom because of the $9.00 ticket. There is more quarreling in families–some discussing "divorce" so the wife and family can receive welfare benefits. Adults scurry for any type of work, including part-time jobs that teens would normally perform. While the displaced worker looks for work, he often finds that his spouse is more employable and he is left at home "to make stew and putter around". Job loss is not the positive experience it was to many in the mid-1970s (Little, 1976; Root, 1978; Strange, 1978). Job loss impacts for blue collar workers

153

are frequently found to be similar to those noted in the *Register* article
and are even worse for those in single-industry communities. Hansen
and Bentley (1981b) quote *The Salt Lake Tribune's* description of some of
these impacts in Anaconda, Montana:

> Property crimes, mental illness, alcohol and drug problems have
> increased dramatically in Anaconda since the Anaconda Copper Co.
> closed its smelter last fall, officials say.
>
> More than 1,000 people were put out of work and the combined
> city-county government lost more than $425,000 in tax revenue when
> the smelter shut down.
>
> Police Chief Dan Jancic said, "It took a little time for the thing to
> hit, but now we're feeling the full effect of it".
>
> The number of calls pertaining to alcohol problems is up 75
> percent, and mental health reports are running 80 percent higher,
> Jancic said. Family disruptions in May and June increased from an
> average of 25 to 50, he said.
>
> The financially strapped local government has been forced to
> lay off police officers, and Jancic said the community's problems can
> only get worse.

The impact of the Anaconda smelter closure for the community is perhaps understood more clearly when we realize that the 1,000 lost jobs
occurred in a community of 12,500 and the $21 million annual payroll the
smelter provided was 80% of the local economy. Even though many
communities are confronted with difficulties when a major employer
closes, energy-related communities may be even more constrained. The
energy resource community is more likely to be in a remote area, does not
often have a diversified economic base and thus fewer local employment
opportunities, and has a workforce with industry-specific skills. The communities themselves may not have a sense of permanence, in part
because of an uneven power structure, and may not have a capable
leadership to respond to the closure.

In this paper I want to sketch out some of the issues confronting
communities involved in a plant closure, noting differences in the consequences of shutdowns for traditional communities and those developed
as energy resource entities. A logical first question is, what do we know
about shutdowns in energy-related communities?

CLOSURE LITERATURE

Although plant shutdowns have been studied rather extensively,
these studies are generally case studies of a single shutdown frequently
focusing on the financial impacts for the worker and his/her family.
Recent bibliographies for the U.S.A. (Root, 1979; Hansen *et al.*, 1982) and

work in progress at York University in Canada by Gerald Hunnius and Paul Grayson have attempted to collate these studies with the aim of expanding research. A search of this literature indicates that few energy resource shutdowns are described. Another relatively recent entrant of bibliographies emphasizes Boom Towns (President's Economic Adjustment Committee, 1981) but the thrust seems to be managing and planning for growth, not for decline.

An attempt to summarize the literature on closures in energy resource communities with the relevant issues in the decommissioning of facilities is not an easy task, largely due to the paucity of references. Fortunately, there are three indirect, and helpful, sources: literature on the decommissioning of military facilities, writings on mining and other resource communities and literature on community reactions to plant closures.

First, the decommissioning of military installations may be used as a proxy for energy-related shutdowns. Frequently, these military installations are in remote smaller communities with heavy reliance upon shopping, recreation, and ancillary services for military base personnel. The literature in this area is extensive, although infrequently cited. Furthermore any generalization from this data base has its limitations, since military installation decommissionings are atypical in several important ways:

1. Military personnel comprise a major portion of the local work force, and are transferred to other posts, leaving housing, decreased demand on local businesses and services, but not the high unemployment rate which would be associated with a civilian workforce;

2. The U.S. Government promotes economic development by selling the land and facilities to local or state governments;

3. The Department of Defense provides experienced decommissioning personnel to assist the local community in redevelopment of the military installation; and

4. The lead time for military closure is often several years in advance of the actual shutdown.

A second source of information about the decline of energy resource communities are brief descriptions and/or case studies of mining communities, supplemented with classics like Robinson's *New Industrial Towns on Canada's Resource Frontier*. Robinson (1962) describes the leap-frog growth of isolated communities solely dependent for their existence upon some resource:

Because these giant resource projects are located in sparsely settled and municipally unorganized areas, they provided the impetus for the construction of townsites that accommodate their workers and famflies. Thus, in the unsettled areas all across the north, new communities have sprung up...Murdockville (in the Gaspe), Schefferville and Seven Islands (in Quebec), Uranium City (in Saskatchewan)...These are only a few of the better known. All told, some forty-six new towns came into being in the period 1945 to 1957, each built around a single resource-based industrial enterprise.

At the other end of the cycle, Robinson describes the dilemma of Kitimat's decline when the aluminum demand diminished and the loss of 1,800 jobs reinforced its single energy resource dependency. Elliot Lake's dependence on uranium was much the same story.

Gordus et al. (1981) note some changes in how communities face a shutdown. Two decades ago communities were reactive; now some communities are proactive. Should a community wait until disaster strikes to develop coordination and mobilization capacities? Still, literature about community response to shutdowns is difficult to locate, and none of the communities involved in a shutdown identified by Gordus and associates deal with energy or mining, and none are single-industry, isolated communities. Their literature search required a strong dependence upon unpublished materials, and tended to emphasize: (1) costs to the community when a shutdown occurs; (2) what happens after a closing, including worker-ownership and other options; and (3) coordination of community services after a shutdown.

A third aid to understanding energy-related shutdowns is the recent manuals on the theme of community response to plant closures. These give specific suggestions and further document the impact of the type of shutdowns described in the literature reviewed by Gordus and her colleagues. These manuals include Hansen and Bentley (1981c), Langerman et al. (1982), Mazza (1982), State of California (1982) and Swerdloff (1980).

Let me proceed with the task of summarizing our admittedly limited knowledge about energy-related shutdowns, raising questions about relevant issues and at least noting the shortfalls in our knowledge. There are five aspects that communities need to consider and work through to reduce the trauma of job loss for displaced workers and to maintain a cohesive community. These are: (1) Timing–Notification and Prenotification; (2) Corporate Integration and Strategy; (3) Community Leadership Skills; (4) Community Industrial Development; and (5) Government Intervention.

SHUTDOWN CONSIDERATIONS

Timing: Notification and Prenotification

There are at least four aspects to the shutdown timing variable. One is whether lead time is provided by the company to the community and the work force. Without question the "springing" of a shutdown without early notice increases frustration and confusion in the work force and does not allow the community any planning time. Many of the state plans for legislation require (or would require) advance notice of shutdown (Gordus *et al.*, 1981, pp. 58-64). A second aspect of the timing is the amount of lead time provided. McKersie and McKersie (1982) indicate that until 1980, only about 10% of collective bargaining agreements required any advance notice, and the time requirements were brief, usually only several weeks or a month. The past two years have seen tremendous growth in the number of agreements with a prenotification clause; 3 to 6 months is the norm.

A third aspect of the timing issue involves the displacement pattern of the shutdown. Whether everyone is displaced at once or whether there is a reduction-in-force over time will influence the impact of the shutdown for both workers and the community. The layoff pattern may be a significant indicator of whether workers will move, or whether they should be encouraged to move.

A final dimension to the shutdown timing problem is its relationship to other community commitments or "problems". For example, the closure of a facility after the community has committed extensive funds for pollution control for this industry is viewed with greater irritation than if the company simply had closed. Likewise, the closure of one facility in a community becomes compounded when it follows on the heels of others and creates an even larger surplus of residents without work.

Given the potential negative impacts if there is no advance warning, some lead time appears desirable. However, advance notice of shutdown in an energy-resource community may generate considerably larger numbers of quits than in a factory where transfer, separation pay, and retirement are fairly standard options. Hansen *et al.* (1980) describe the closure of The Park City Ventures mine in Park City, Utah, in mid-February, 1978 and the Burgin Mine located near Eureka, Utah, which was owned and operated by Kennecott Copper Corporation. The Burgin mine, with 150 workers, was closed July 15, 1978, but the announcement to close came just one month earlier. Within that month, three-fifths of the workers quit their jobs, perhaps to get a head start on the job search.

Corporate Integration and Strategy

Whether the company involved in a shutdown is a locally owned operation, a multiplant national organization, or an international enterprise will make a difference to company efforts and involvement at the community level, commitment to local concerns, and the availability of personnel in accessing governmental assistance programs. For example, the size and integration of Chrysler Corporation and the anticipated ripple effects of closure may have been crucial ingredients in determining Chrysler's successful guaranteed government loan.

But energy-related communities are often in remote areas, and several of the older communities started as mining camps. Coal Town is one example, "Initially conceived in 1900 as a privately owned, unincorporated camp, dominated and controlled by the six Basil brothers who had pooled their individual resources in order to speculate in coal" (Lantz, 1958).

The Bisbee, Arizona, copper mine, owned by Phelps-Dodge Corporation is another example. The Bisbee mine had a reduction-in-force from 1,200 to 100 when the open pit shut down and all underground mining operations were terminated in 1975. As a community of 8,600, Bisbee was a company town focussing on copper mining and owed its existence to a copper mining camp started in 1878. Twenty-two weeks after the first layoff, Martin et al. (1976) found "about one-fourth of the workers were rehired, about one-fourth left town and/or found other jobs in the area, and about one-half of the workers remain unemployed in Bisbee."

The Bisbee analysis described young truck drivers as more mobile and easily reemployed. Anglos with construction work experience had an advantage over their Mexican-American counterparts while limited-skill Mexican-Americans were favored in other mining positions. Although early retirement was an option, no mention of transfer as a shutdown alternative was made.

The degree to which energy-related industries have a sense of corporate responsibility or local community commitment will significantly influence their willingness to provide transfers, assist in the retraining effort, provide employment counselling and motivation sessions, extend health care benefits, or even renegotiate increased benefits for the soon-to-be-terminated workers (Teague, 1980). This same commitment will extend beyond the worker and determine the degree to which the corporation will become involved as a significant actor in the community, not only in the effort to assist displaced workers, but in providing support for industrial development and making land or buildings available to the community for new industry. This ethos of community commitment or corporate responsibility applies equally well to all industries, not just to those which are energy-related.

A corporate strategy might include shouldering the task of aiding workers in locating new employment. Sometimes referred to as "the Company Model", this is probably the most desirable mode of handling a shutdown, both from the standpoint of the affected workers and the community. It is a desirable option because the company is involved in all phases of concern and programming for their soon-to-be-displaced workers. It can commit the resources to make the program successful, and it can most effectively merchandise the skills of their workers. The company makes a substantial statement to both the workers and the community when they meet this responsibility, and they simultaneously free up community leadership for industrial development or to provide ancillary resources.

Two closures, neither in energy-related industries, illustrate the company model. The Brown and Williamson Tobacco Corporation closure of its Louisville facility, displacing 3000 workers, was a gradual phase-out over nearly three years (McKersie and McKersie, 1982). Planning for the shutdown was guided by three basic company principles: (1) advance notification, (2) joint involvement between labor and management in the shutdown process, and (3) gradual reduction of the work force. In addition to transfer rights, early retirement, and extended medical coverage for six months after job loss, Brown and Williamson involved its workers in employment counselling, assisted workers in creating resumes, sought employment for their employees in other industries throughout Kentucky through mailings, and provided company facilities and time off for employees to be interviewed. High school classes and the GED equivalency test were made available on company premises. Retraining through company-financed outside programs was also available. Comparable programs were provided to Dana Corporation employees in Edgerton, Wisconsin, where the workforce of nearly 1600 dropped to 300 in a six-month period before the announcement to close was made in May, 1980 (McKersie and McKersie, 1982). The Dana program was guided by company-based policies: (1) displaced Dana workers should be primary candidates for openings at other Dana facilities, with eligibility lasting for five years beyond the layoff date, and two months pay for relocation expenses, and (2) a major effort to create a Job Search Program, including a Job Search Center with a microfilm system and telephones. Through the Job Search Program, Dana announced the availability of their workers to over 3000 companies in the southern Wisconsin and northern Illinois area. Although the Dana Job Search Center worked closely with the Wisconsin Job Service, Dana kept its placement efforts separate to avoid the backlog to the State Job Service Office.

Community Leadership Skills

How the community organizes in response to either an announcement or a closure depends on the interest and skills of local government,
business, and service provider leaders. Although "the Company model"
for closure may only minimally involve community leaders and local
government agencies, that model is infrequently available, and the community must take the initiative in responding to the closure. Three options
exist for the community: The Community Model, A Segmented Model,
and The Community Disorganization Model.

The Community Model is probably the most common effort to assist
displaced workers. This model involves a set of actors representing the
company, union, service agencies, religious organizations, educational
centers, employment services, etc. to coordinate a planned attack in assisting the displaced workers and/or recruiting new industry. It can be
very effective in creating a sense of community spirit when a community
has confronted a problem with resolve and success.

The Des Moines, Iowa effort to assist nearly 1,000 workers displaced
in the fall of 1981 when Wilson Foods and Massey Ferguson closed their
Des Moines operations, is a good example of the community model
requiring involvement of community leaders in an organized manner
(Langerman et al., 1982). Des Moines, with funding from a variety of
sources, including Massey Ferguson, created a "Mayor's Task Force on
Plant Closing and Job Retraining" which not only created the publicity
and focus on new employment or retraining for the displaced workers,
but also created two Transition Centers. The Transition Centers were
staffed by paid full-time displaced workers who helped their out-of-work
colleagues with applications for Unemployment Insurance and CETA,
assessed skills and work interests, provided employment and financial
counselling, made referrals to supportive services and counselling, provided job referrals or job referrals through Job Service offices, gave
referrals to retraining programs and assisted in developing job search
workshops. While the Transition Centers were open for customers, other
sub-committees of the Task Force were involved in preparing a brochure
of community services, identifying the retraining needs and funding
sources, as well as focusing on job development and placement for the
displaced workers.

A Segmented Model, comprised of elements of the affected community, exists when neither the entire community joins in the effort or
when there are factions of the community working simultaneously, but
independently, in assistance efforts. The segmented model frequently
involves the union, or worker representatives, aligned with a ministerial
association, and/or with job service. Missing are business and govern-

ment leaders, and often underriding the lackluster program are under-
tones of factions which are unwilling to join together in a common effort.
Since government and business leadership are important segments in the
community models and may be missing in the segmented models, the
effort gets less than total commitment. Since retraining and industrial
development grants are often written out of the Mayor's Office, a shortage of involvement from that quarter is a serious blow to the success of
the efforts of those in the community seeking to organize.

The segmented model, or anything short of the company or community models, puts greater strain on displaced workers, particularly workers
who are ill-prepared for job loss. Bendick (1981) maintains that displaced
coal miners suffer a clear disadvantage in obtaining new employment
because of their educational deficiencies. Coal mine workers have at-
tained a median of 8.1 years of complete schooling, compared to the 11.3
years for the U.S. blue-collar worker, and 10.5 years by the U.S. nonfarm
laborer. Both the credential of a high school diploma and fundamental
literacy are major handicaps in the coal miner's job search. Although he
is not an advocate of retraining for miners, Bendick suggests that retraining should provide basic literacy skills and allow displaced miners the
opportunity to obtain high-school equivalency credentials and thus
substantially improve their reemployment prognosis.

The Community Disorganization Model is a "no effort" or uncoordinated program which suggests dismal failure to either retrain employees
or to handle the problems associated with the closure. Rothstein's 1953
account could probably be duplicated in many communities today:

> The relocation of the Babcock plant directly affected the individual
> worker and his family, the firm itself, the city government, the union,
> and the merchants of the community. Yet it was apparent that none of
> the parties involved had more than a vague comprehension of the
> consequences of the plant's relocation. As a result there were many
> serious blocks to the concensus need for concerted action, not only
> between groups but within each group as well.
>
> Lack of concensus on the part of subgroups within each group
> resulted in internal disagreements not only as to means and proce-
> dures but even regarding the nature of the goals themselves. Needed
> action was too little and too late. The City Council, for example, did
> not take a step in regards to rezoning which would have kept the
> Babcock Company (with its wages and taxes) in New London. The
> union was unable to decide whether the offer of a general wage
> decrease was preferable to having the firm move. The retail mer-
> chants never exerted their full potential pressure on the City Council
> to act.

Lack of knowledge both as to consequences and as to means of getting consensus, therefore, played a large role in failing to keep the Babcock Company in New London. Conferences between the company and city officials and the company and union officials did occur, but at no time did the several parties genuinely cooperate to solve the problem.

At least one closure manual (Mazza, 1982) suggests that "the closing jarred local and state leaders into action that was perhaps long overdue". But what about those communities that are not stirred to respond? Are resource towns developed to meet the company's extraction goals and then abandoned when those resources are depleted?

Hansen and Bentley (1981a) report there was a serious gap on the part of personnel and agencies which should be well informed about plant shutdowns, and these agencies were not able to provide advice and leadership in dealing with these events as they occur. As a result, the task of organizing the community was more difficult and time-consuming than anticipated.

In describing the PCV shutdown and the Burgin Mine closure, Hansen *et al.* (1980) note some community differences, but surprisingly similar failures in community support. The PCV shutdown displaced 350 residents, while the 150 Burgin Mine employees were scattered throughout several communities and the county, " . . . so the impact of the shutdown was hardly felt in the nearby town of Eureka". In terms of community response:

The plight of the workers in both cases was an individual plight. There was no response by political or other leaders in the affected communities to organize on a community-wide basis to help ameliorate the serious consequence of the shutdown for the workers and their families. While this is partly understandable in the case of the Burgin Mine, which was located in a rural sparsely inhabited area with no nearby community, still there was no effort made by the Utah County Commissioners to lead out in helping organize a community response. In the case of PCV, neither the immediate communities of Park City or Heber City, nor the Summit County Commissioners responded in the face of the impending shutdown. In our judgment such efforts were both warranted and would have measurably improved the success of the readjustment process. And, the employers at Burgin and Park City responded in the traditional way with regard to the plight of their displaced workers–minimally and somewhat reluctantly (Hansen *et al.*, 1980, pp. 88-89).

The variety of community organization models and their unequal outcomes suggests that how a community organizes its response to a closure will provide an opportunity to fulfill a ghost-town prophecy or alternatively, a commitment and sense of vitality for residents if effective community planning is possible. Access to non-local specialists or consultants, the availability of the to-be-abandoned property, and the degree to which the employer is obliged to share in the burden of change and work with the community will also help determine the success of an organized community effort.

Community Industrial Development

Economic development is an important ingredient in providing the labor demand for a community and, although great variation in the success of communities exists, the response effort to a closure can be a real turnaround (Hansen and Bentley, 1981b). Some communities respond: "We're more cohesive, better organized, more diversified, and more successful at getting even more industries." Others reply that it is too difficult to get industry to take a look at their community.

In military decommissioning, the ultimate responsibility for determining the final base reuse rests with the community leadership and, given good leadership and community organization, defense base closings provide an opportunity to prompt new industrial development, provide improved public services, and stimulate long-term economic growth. To substantiate this claim for the Department of Defense, the following data are provided:

A total of 78,765 civilian jobs has been generated on the 75 former Defense facilities as of February, 1977, replacing the loss of 68,800 DOD civilian or contractor jobs. Industrial parks had been established at 47 of the former bases; three others were being operated as private sector industrial plants. Thirty-one of the former bases were being used as municipal or general aviation airports. Seven four-year colleges and 26 post-secondary vocational-technical institutes had been established at the former bases with 52,512 students. Another 4,215 secondary vo-tech students and 5,309 trainees were also receiving education and training at the former Defense bases. The experience of the previously impacted communities demonstrates that former Defense bases do have a *significant civilian reuse potential when properly planned and redeveloped.*

Anticipation of the closure in the Bisbee mining area and nearby Douglas, Arizona, smelting operations were already in the planners' notes in 1972, three years before closure (Layton and Ayer, 1972). In anticipation of single-industry shutdowns in these communities close to the Mexican border, redevelopment was considered in three modes: tourism, retirement settlement and manufacturing. Layton and Ayer summarize their response to these alternatives:

* Our estimates indicate that the effect of mine-smelter phase-down may have sharp repercussions on population, employment, and gross county product of the local economy. Furthermore, attempts to alleviate these impacts, whether by increased tourism, retirement settlment, or manufacturing, are unlikely to meet this goal. For public officials or planners interested in the welfare of the citizens of these communities, we suggest that they include in their repertoire of programs ones to help residents move out of the region.

Dean's (1965) description of Minersville, a declining one-industry coal mining town, as a community which would not be receptive to redevelopment because of "a) insularity; b) alienation; and c) langour" suggests that community residents themselves need to identify the problem before support for community organization exists.

Government Intervention

Yet another consideration in assessing the dynamics of shutdowns includes government intervention. In Norway, Vatne's work (1980, 1981) describes government involvement in mature single-industry energy communities, reflecting a society-accepted (and expected) role of local-state intervention to prevent ghost-towns. Government intervention strategies in closures from several industrial countries cover a spectrum which includes guaranteed loans, performance loans, tax benefits, subsidized production, and feasibility studies to determine the possibility of a worker-owned industry.

At least one study of a U.S. community showed that long term government support, especially if uncoordinated, is not the complete answer for any community (Gordus et al., 1981). Emphasis from several sources (Gordus, 1981; President's Economic Adjustment Committee, 1978; Amos and Rumburg, 1980) indicates that communities must themselves perceive the problem, mobilize resources and develop coordination to implement a plan best fitted to that community's situation. Community leaders must then win the support of community members to carry out that plan.

Although the traditional energy-resource community was generally developed by a private company, more public involvement in the planning of these communities has recently taken place. In Quebec, provincial government administrators of both the Ministries of Mines and Municipal Affairs have long held control over the development of new towns (Robinson, 1962). In Alberta, New Town Legislation provides development assistance and Detomasi (1979) notes that decentralization of either population and/or economic activity may breathe new life in smaller energy dependent communities whose demise was certain.

There are large gaps in our knowledge of the influence of political decisions on plant closures. For example, we do not have empirical studies of how those who hold community power and influence might sway the outcome of community response to a shutdown or bring their influence to bear in preventing or ameliorating a closure. Are there community leaders (bankers, lawyers or real estate agents) interested in promoting a shutdown for their own advantage? We lack empirical insight into the corporate decision-making process of shutting down a facility or deciding to remain in a community when there appear to be several equally attractive communities in which to relocate a facility. We simply do not know where incentives work, at what costs or for how long. Why do energy-related communities (or any community for that matter) not plan for an eventual decline? They leave themselves open to dwindling resources, tremendous technological change or volatile economic conditions that may render yesterday's major industry tomorrow's plant closure.

CONCLUSION

We need to remind ourselves that the crisis of a plant closure is real, for workers, for their families, and for communities in which that shutdown occurs. That crisis is often more traumatic in hard times like the present, when it is difficult for workers to find new employment. That crisis is more traumatic for many energy-related communities because they are in remote locations and depend heavily on one industry. If resources are slim for redevelopment and a diversified economic base is non-existent, worker residents may be quick to leave. When the community is larger and more diversified, with an integrated economic base, like Calgary, Canada, or Stavanger, Norway, the community impact of a shutdown will obviously be different. We have much to learn about energy resource communities and much to discover about their diversity.

Government intervention, greater awareness of quality-of-life issues, community organization expertise from residents, and an increased concern for societal planning in some countries reflect concern for energy resource communities and their resident populations. Not many of us are excited to see our own community, or one nearby, become famous (or infamous) as a societal pocket of high unemployment.

Energy-resource communities are often characterized as single-industry towns whose existence depends on the extraction or processing of a natural resource which cannot be expected to last forever. Even if the resource lasts for several generations, market trends, new technology, transportation costs, plant/mine efficiency and labor costs, as well as the condition of the facility, are all significantly variable to suggest that planning for the end of the production cycle may be as significant as front-end planning. So far, little planning for mature energy-resource communities has taken place.

Literature Cited

Aiken, Michael and Robert R. Alford, 1974. "Community structure and innovation: public housing, urban renewal and the War on Poverty", pp. 231-287 in Terry N. Clark (ed.), *Comparative Community Politics* (New York: Wiley-Halsted).

Albrecht, S., 1978. "Socio-cultural Factors and Energy Resource Development in Rural Areas in the West" *Journal of Environmental Management*, 7: 78-90.

Albrecht, Stan and Pamela Bergmann, 1982. *Price Community Report: BLM Social Effects Project* (Billings, MT: Mountain West Research, Inc.).

Alford, Robert R., 1974. *The Political Economy of Health Care* (Chicago: University of Chicago Press).

Amos, J.M. and W.S. Rumburg, 1980 *Effects of the Loss of St. Joseph Minerals Corporation as a Major Employer on St. Fraccois County. Missouri* Center for Applied Engineering Management, University of Missouri-Rolla.

Andrews, W.H. and W.W. Bauder, 1968. *Comparison of Social Change in Monroe and Noble Counties of Ohio* Department Series AE407 (Wooster OH: Ohio Agricultural Research and Development Center).

Anonymous, 1981. "Socioeconomic Impact Mitigation Agreement for the Deserado Mine, Bonanza Station and Associated Facilities" Mimeograph, June.

Anonymous, 1982. "More or Less Oil Will Go Up or Down or Maybe It Won't" *Wall Street Journal*, 9 May, p. 2.

Architectural Forum, 1954. "Industry Builds Kitimat–First Complete New Town in North America", *Architectural Forum*, July, pp. 128-147.

Aronson, C., 1981. *Energy Development in Rural Areas: Corporate Provision of Housing and Community Infrastructure* (Seattle WA: Battelle Human Affairs Research Center).

Baffin Region Inuit Association, 1979. *Socio-Economic Impacts of the Nanisivik Mine on Northern Baffin Region Communities, Frobisher Bay, NWT* Baffin Region Inuit Association unpublished study, on file with the Department of Indian Affairs and Northern Development.

Banfield, E.C. and J.Q. Wilson, 1963. *City Politics* (Cambridge: Harvard University Press and M.I.T. Press).

Banfield, Edward C., 1965. *Political Influence: A New Theory of Urban Politics* (New York: Free Press).

Barrows, R. and M. Charlier, 1980. "Local government options for managing rapid growth in rural areas: the case of boomtown growth from mining and energy facilities" Paper presented to the Seminar on Coping with Rapid Growth, Scottsdale, Arizona.

Beck, E.M., 1972. "Industrial Development and Occupational Movers and Stayers" Working Paper RID 72.17, Dept. of Rural Sociology, U. of Wisconsin-Madison.

Bender, L.D., B.L. Green and R.R. Campbell, 1971. "Trickle-down and Leakage in the War on Poverty" *Growth and Change*, Vol. 2, No. 4.

Bendick, M. Jr., 1981. *Assisting Coal Miners Dislocated by Sulfur Emissions Restrictions: Issues and Options* (Washington DC: The Urban Institute).

Berg, P.O., 1965. *Ringvirkninger av ny Stor Industri Utbikling i Naerngsliv og Bosetting i Ardal og Mo i Rama med Omliggende Distriker Siden 1946* Publikasjan Nr. 1 (Oslo: Distriktenes Utbyggingsfund).

Berge, A. and A. O /vsthus, 1975. *Rekruttering av Arbeids-Kraft til Mongstad Anlegget* (Bergen: Norwegian School of Economics and Business Administration).

Berkey, E., N.G. Carpenter, W.C. Metz, D.W. Myers, D.R. Portes, J.E. Singley, and R.K. Travis, 1977. *Social Impact Assessment, Monitoring and Management by the Electric Energy Industry* (Pittsburgh, PA: Energy Impact Associates, Inc.).

Betz, Marga R., "Community Stability in Resource Towns: Problems and Potentials", unpublished, 1980, Calgary.

Beveridge, J. and R. Schindelka, 1980. *Proposed "B" Zone Development at Rabbit Lake: Assessment of Northern Community Impact* Unpublished study. (Saskatoon: Institute for Northern Studies, University of Saskatchewan).

Black, T.R., C. Fredrickson and S.T. Maitland, 1960. *Industrialization of Box Elder County* (Logan, Utah: Utah State University).

Bloomquist, L.E. and G.F. Summers, 1982. "Organization of Production and Community Income Distribution" *American Sociological Review* (forthcoming).

Bodley, J.H., 1975. *Victims of Progress* (Menlo Park, CA: Cummings Publishing Co.).

Bowles, R.T., 1981. *Social Impact Assessment in Small Communities* (Toronto: Butterworths).

Bradbury, J. H. "Instant Resource Towns Policy in British Columbia, 1965-1972", *Plan Canada*, VOl. 20, No. 1 (March 1980), 19-38.

Bradbury, J.H., "Towards an Alternative Theory of Resource Based Town Development in Canada", *Economic Geography* 55 (1979), 147-66.

Bradshaw, T.K. and E.J. Blakely, 1979. *Rural Communities in Advanced Industrial Society: Development and Developers* (New York: Praeger).

Brady, Guy Jr., 1974. *The Economic Impact of Industrialization on a Rural Town Economy: Wynne, Arkansas* (Fayettevill AR: The University of Arkansas).

Briscoe, Maphis, Murray and Lamont, Inc., 1978. *Action Handbook: Managing Growth in the Small Community* (Boulder, CO: Prepared for U.S. Environmental Protection Agency).

Brookshire, D. and D'Arge, R., "Adjustment Issues of Impacted Communities or, Are Boomtowns Bad?" *Natural Resources Journal* 20 (1980).

Buckley, W., 1967. *Sociology and Modern Systems Theory* (Englewood Cliffs, NJ: Prentice-Hall, Inc.).

Bulmer, M., 1975. "Sociological Models of the Mining Community" *Sociological Review*, 23, p. 61-92.

Bureau of Population and Economic Research, 1956. *The Impact of Industry in a Southern Rural County* Bureau of Population and Economic Research, University of Virginia (Richmond, VA: Virginia Department of Highways).

Burvill, P.W., "Mental Health in Isolated New Mining Towns in Australia", *Australian and New Zealand Journal of Psychiatry*, 9:77 (1978).

Canning, S. and G. Inglis, 1979. "But Will it Make Sope? Prospects for Offshore Petroleum Development in Newfoundland" in J. Sewel (ed.) *The Promise and the Reality–Large Scale Development in Marginal Regions* (Aberdeen: Institute for the Study of Sparsely Populated Areas).

Carcajou Research Limited, 1980. *Final report of the Grande Prairie Region Community Impact Study–1980* (Edmonton: Northern Alberta Development Council).

Castells, Manuel (ed.), 1973. *Imperilismo y Urbanizacion en America Latino* (Barcelona: Gustavo Gili).

Castells, Manuel, 1972. *La Question Urbaine* (Paris: Librairie Francois Maspero).

Champion, D. and Ford, A., 1980. "Boom-Town Effects" *Environment*, Vol. 22, 5, p. 25-31.

Choukron, J.M. and Jacob, A.L., "Financing New Communities: Problems and Prospects" in *New Communities in Canada: Exploring Planned Environments* N. Pressman, ed. *Contact* 8, No. 3 (Special Issue, 1976) 137-45.

Clark, T.N., 1967. "Power and community structure: who governs, where, and when? *The Sociological Quarterly*, 8 (Summer): 291-316.

Clark, T.N., 1968. "Who governs, where, when, and with what effects? pp. 15-23 in T.N. Clark (ed.), *Community Structure and Decision-Making: Comparative Analyses* (San Francisco: Chandler Publishing Company).

Clement, F. and G.F. Summers, 1973a. "Industrial Development and the Elderly: A Longitudinal Analysiš *Journal of Gerontology*, Vol. 28, No. 4, pp. 479-483.

Clement, W., 1978. "A Political Economy of Regionalism in Canadă pp. 89-110 in D. Glenday, H. Guindon and Turowetz (eds.) *Modernization and the Canadian State* (Toronto: MacMillan).

Clement, W., 1981. *Hard-Rock Mining: Industrial Relations and Technological Changes at Inco* (Toronto: McClelland and Stewart).

Clemente, F. and G.F. Summers, 1973b. "Large Industries in Small Towns: Who Benefits? Working Paper RID 73.9 (Madison WI: Center of Applied Sociology, University of Wisconsin-Madison).

Cohen, R., 1962. *An Anthropoligical Survey of Communities in the Mackenzie-Slave Lake Region of Canada* (Ottawa: Department of Northern Affairs and Natural Resources).

Coon, R.C., N. Dalsted, A.G. Leholm and F.L. Leistritz, 1976. *The Impact of the Safeguard Antiballistic Missile System Construction on Northeastern North Dakota* Ag. Ec. Rpt. 101, Dept. of Agric. Econ. (Fargo, ND: North Dakota State University).

Copes, P., 1972. *Resettlement of Fishing Communities in Newfoundland* (Ottawa: Canadian Council on Rural Development).

Cortese, C.F. and B. Jones, 1977. "The sociological analysis of boomtownš *Western Socioogical Review*, 8 (i):76-90.

Crain, R.L. and D.B. Rosenthal, 1967. "Community Status as a dimension in local decision-makiñ *American Sociological Review*, 32 (December): 970-984.

Crenson, M.A., 1971. *The Un-Politics of Air Pollution* (Baltimore: Johns Hopkins University Press).

Cummings, R.G., and Mehr, A., "Investments for Urban Infrastructure in Boomtownš *Natural Resources Journal* 17 (1977), 221-40.

DRAND, 1980. "Preliminary Assessment of Impacts of Oil and Gas Development on Rural Development in Newfoundland and Labradoř Newfoundland Department of Rural, Agricultural and Northern Development mimeo.

DREE, n.d. *Single Industry Communities in Canada* (Ottawa: Department of Regional Economic Expansion).

Davenport, J. and Davenport, J.A., 1981. "Boom Town Victims: Social Work's Latest Clients *Journal of Sociology and Social Welfare*, 8, pp. 150-163.

Davenport, J. and J.A. Davenport (eds.), 1980. *The Boomtown: Problems and Promises in the Energy Vortex* (Laramie, WY: University of Wyoming, Department of Social Work).

Davis, J.N. Jr., 1963. *Effects of Industrialization upon the Economy of Searcy, Arkansas: A Case Study* Ph.D. Dissertation (Fayettevill, AR: University of Arkansas).

DePape, Denis, 1982. "Government/Industry Agreements for Resource Development: Socioeconomic Considerations Presentation to CIM Annual General Meeting, Quebec City, Quebec, April 27.

Dean, L., 1965. "Minersville: A Study of Socioeconomic Stagnation *Human Organization*, 24(Fall): 254-261.

Deaton, B.J. and M.R. Landes, 1978. "Rural Industrialization and the Changing Distribution of Family Incomes *American Journal of Agricultural Economics*, Vol. 60, No. 5, pp. 950-954.

Deaton, B.J., 1979. "Industrialization of Rural Areas: Recent Trends and the Social and Economic Consequences Staff Paper SP-79-5 (Blacksburg VA: Virginia Polytechnic and State University).

Denver Research Institute, 1979. *Case Studies: Socioeconomic Impacts of Western Energy Resource Development* Vol II, June.

Detomasi, D.D., "The Growth of Small Towns: The Special Case of Boom Towns in *Small Town Alberta: Some Points of View on Growth and Development* Proceedings of a Conference held in Banff Park Lodge, March 11-14, 1979. Sponsors: The Faculty of Extension; The University of Alberta; The Faculty of Continuing Education; The University of Lethbridge and The Faculty of Extension, The University of Calgary.

Detomasi, D.D., 1979. "The Decentralization of Population and/or Economic Activity: A Method for Assessing Its Impact on Small Centers pp. 76-89 in W.T. Perks and I.M. Robinson (eds.) *Urban and Regional Planning in a Federal State: The Canadian Experience* (New York: McGraw-Hill Book Co.).

Dixon, Mim, 1978. *What Happened to Fairbanks? The Effects of the Trans-Alaska Oil Pipeline on the Community of Fairbanks, Alaska* (Boulder, CO: Westview Press).

Duncan, R.B., 1979. "Characteristics of organizational environments and perceived environmental uncertainty pp. 42-58 in M. Zay-Ferrell (ed.) *Readings on Dimensions of Organizations: Environment, Context, Structure, Process, and Performance* (Santa Monica, CA: Goodyear).

Dye, T.R., 1968. *Urban school segregation: a comparative analysis*, Urban Affairs Quarterly, 4 (December): 141-164

ECC, 1980 (Economic Council of Canada). *Newfoundland: From Dependency to Self-Reliance* (Hull, PQ: Ministry of Supply and Services).

Eskedal, L., 1979. *Leveranser til Rafinor A/S 1974 og Vedlikeholds Utigifter 1975-77* Notat Nr. 5/79 (Bergen: Inst. of Industrial Economics).

FEPA, Maksymak & Associates Limited, Roy Fletchr, Study Director, Ira M. Robinson Consultant. *Alternative Approaches to the Planning and Development of Canadian Resource Communities: Inventory and Final Reports* Prepared for the Ministry of State for Urban Affairs, Urban Policy Analysis Branch, Ottawa: MSUA, October, 1977.

Faas, R.C., 1982. *Evaluation of Impact Mitigation Strategies: Case Studies of Four Tax-Exempt Facilities* (Corvallis OR: Western Rural Development Center).

Fainstein, N.I. and S.S. Fainstein, 1974. *Urban Political Movements: The Search for Power by Minortiy Groups in American Cities* (Englewood Cliff, NJ: Prentice-Hall).

Finsterbusch, K., 1980. *Understanding Social Impacts: Assessing the Effects of Public Projects* (London: Sage Publications).

Funk, H., 1964. "The Effects of New Manufacturing Plant on Business Firms in an Eastern Iowa Community" Ph.D. Dissertation, Dept. of Economics, Iowa State University.

Garth, J., 1953. "Whe Big Business Comes to a Country Town: Why ALCOA Spent

Gartrell, J.W. and Krahn, H., 1980b. *Cold Lake Regional Baseline Study, Phase II* (Edmonton: Northern Development Branch, Alberta Small Business and Tourism).

Gartrell, J.W., 1979. *A Study of Human Adjustment in Fort McMurray* HS 30.5, A Report for AOSERP (Edmonton: U. of Alberta, Population Research Lab.).

Gartrell, J.W., 1982. "Community as a Social Collective" pp. 199-218 in Summers and Selvik (eds.) *Energy Resource Communities* (Madison, WI: MJM Publishing Co.).

Gartrell, J.W., Krahn, H. and Sunahara, F.D., 1980a. *A Study of Human Adjustment in Fort McMurray* (Edmonton: Alberta Oil Sands Environmental Research Program, Alberta Environment).

Gigot, P., 1982. "Even in a Small Iowa City, Slump Hits Some Hard but Spares Others" *The Wall Street Journal*, Friday, May 7.

Gilmore, J.S. and M.K. Duff, 1975. *Boom Town Growth Management: A Case Study of Rock Springs-Green River, Wyoming* (Boulder, CO: Westview Press).

Gilmore, J.S, 1976. "Boomtowns may hinder energy resource development" *Science,* Vol. 191 (February).

Gilmore, J.S., D. Hammond, K. Moore, J. Johnson and D. Coddington, 1981. *Socioeconomic Impacts of Power Plants* Report prepared for Electric Power Research Insitute (Denver CO: Denver Research Institute).

Gilmore, J.S., K.D. Moore, D.M. Hammond and D.C. Coddington, 1976. *Analysis of Financing Problems of Coal and Oil Shale Boom Towns* (Washington DC: Federal Energy Administration).

Gjesteland, D., 1973. *Storbedrift: et Utkantdistrikt. En Analyse av Rekruttering og Yrkestabilitet Blant Ansatte ved Ardal Verk 1646-71* Rapport Nr. 4 (Oslo: Inst. for Sociologi, Ardalsprojecktet).

Goffman, E., 1961. *Asylums* (New York: Anchor).

Gold, R.L., 1979. "On Local Control of Western Energy Development" *The Social Science Journal,* April Vol. 16, No. 2., 121-127.

Goldthorpe, J.H., D. Lockwood, and J. Platt, 1969. *The Affluent Worker in the Class Structure* (Cambridge: Cambridge University Press).

Gordus, J.P., P. Jarley and L.A. Ferman, 1981. *Plant Closings and Economic Dislocation* (Kalamazoo, MI: The W.E. Upjohn Institute for Employment Research).

Gotsch, C.H., 1972. "Technical Change and the Distribution of Income in Rural Areas" *American Journal of Agricultural Economics,* Vol. 54, No. 2, pp 326-341.

Gray, I., 1969. "Employment Effect of a New Industry in a Rural Area" *Monthly Labor Review,* Vol. 92, No. 6, 26-30.

Gray, R., 1962. "Community Impact of New Industry" *Arkansas Economist,* Vol. 4, No. 3.

Greene, M. and M.G. Curry, 1977. *The Management of Social and Economic Impacts Associated with the Construction of Large-Scale Projects: Experiences from the Western Coal Development Community* (Richland WA: Battelle Human Affairs Research Centers, Pacific Northwest Laboratories).

Greenstone, J.D. and P.E. Peterson, 1973. *Race and Authority in Urban Politics* (New York: Russell Sage).

Gunder, M.R.J., 1980. *Resource Community Bibliography* (Vancouver: Simon Fraser U., unpublished).

Hage, J. and M. Aiken, 1967. "Program change and organizational properties: a comparative analysis" *American Journal of Sociology,* 72 (March): 503-519.

Halstead, J.M., F.L. Leistritz, D. G. Rice, D.M. Saxowsky and R.A. Chase, 1982. *Mitigating Socioeconomic Impacts of Nuclear Wast Repository Siting* (Fargo ND: North Dakota Agricultural Experiment Station).

Hannah, R. and R.K. Mosier, 1977. *An Examination of Occupational Bottlenecks in the Construction, Fueling and Operation of Coal-Fired Power Plants* (Salt Lake City UT: University of Utah).

Hansen, G.B. and M.T. Bentley, 1981a. *Mobilizing Community Resources to Cope with Plant Shutdowns: A Demonstration Project* Final Report (Logan UT: Utah State University).

Hansen, G.B. and M.T. Bentley, 1981b. *Problems and Solutions in a Plant Shutdown: A Handbook for Commuity Involvement* (Logan UT: Utah Center for Productivity and Quality of Working Life, Utah State University).

Hansen, G.B. and M.T. Bentley, and Richard A. Davidson, 1980. *Hardrock Miners in a Shutdown: A Case Study of the Post-Layoff Experiences of Displace Lead-Zinc-Silver Miners* (Logan UT: Economic Research Center and Center for Productivity and Quality of Working Life, Utah State University).

Hansen, G.B., M.T. Bentley and M.H. Skidmore, 1981. *Plant Shutdowns, People and Communities: A Selected Bibliography* (Logan UT: Utah Center for Productivity and Quality of Working Life, Utah State University).

Hansen, G.B., M.T. Bentley, and M.H. Skidmore, 1981. *Plant Shutdown, People and Communities: A Selected Bibliography* (Logan UT: Utah State University, Center for Productivity and Quality of Working Life).

Harvey, D., 1973. *Social Justice and the City* (Baltimore: John Hopkins University Press).

Hawley, A.H., 1963. "Community power structure and urban renewal success" *American Journal of Sociology*, 68 (January): 422-431.

Hayes, E.C., 1972. *Power Structure and Urban Policy* (New York: McGraw-Hill).

Healy, R.G., "Effects of Improved Housing on Worker Performance", *Journal of Human Resources*, 6, 277-308.

Helgeson, D.L. and M.J. Zink, 1973. *A Case Study of Rural Industrialization in Jamestown, North Dakota* Ag. Econ. report No. 95, Dept. of Agric, Econ. (Fargo ND: North Dakota State University).

Helm, J. and N.O. Lurie, 1961. *The Subsistence Economy of the Dogrib Indians of Lac la Martre in the Mackenzie District of the N.W.T. Canada* (Ottawa: Department of Northern Affairs and Natural Resources).

Hitzhusen, F. and T. Napier, 1978. "A rural public services policy framework and some applications" pp. 127-149 in *Rural Policy Research Alternatives* (Ames, Iowa: Iowa State University press).

Hobart, C.W. and George Kupfer, 1973. *Inuit Employment of Gulf Oil Canada, Assessment and Impact on Coppermine, 1972-1973* Unpublished study (Edmonton: Westrede Institute).

Hobart, C.W., 1976. *Rotation Work Schedules in the Northwest Territories* (Yellowknife, NWT: Government of the Northwest Territories, Department of Economic Development and Tourism).

Hobart, C.W., 1982. "Industrial Employment of Rural Indigenes: The Case of Canada" *Human Organization*, 41: 54-63.

Hobart, C.W., forthcoming. *Employment and Aftermath: Effects of Oil Industry Employment on a Small Inuit Community* (Edmonton: University of Alberta, Boreal Institute).

Hodge, Gerald, "Age and the Resource Frontier", *Bulleting of the Conservation Council of Ontario*, Vol. 20, No. 3, July 1973.

Hooper, D. and K. Branch, 1982. *Forsyth Community Report: BLM Social Effects Project* (Billings, MT: Mountain West Research, Inc.).

Hooper, D. and P. Jobes, 1982. *Ashland Community Report: BLM Social Effects Project* (Billings, MT: Mountain West Research, Inc.).

Horsfall, R.B. et al., 1974. *Paramenters of Healthful Community and Individual Living in Resource Frontier Towns* (Vancouver: Simon Fraser U.).

House, 1981 is also referred to in Gartrell, but is not in bibliography.

House, J.D., 1980. "Coastal Labrador, Incorporation, Exploration, and Underdevelopment" *Journal of Canadian Studies*, 15, pp. 98-113.

Hunter, F.A., 1953. *Community Power Structure* (Chapel Hill: University of North Carolina Press).

Hushak, L.J., 1979. "Definition and Estimation of Private Sector Benefits" pp. 1-16 in Hushak and Morse (eds.) *Proceedings of the Ex Ante Growth Impact Models Conference* (Ames IA: Iowa State University)

Hutt, W.H., 1934. "The Economic Position of the Bantu in South Africa" pp.195-237 in E. Schapera (ed.) *Western Civilization and the Natives of South Africa* (London: George Routledge and Sons, Ltd.)

Inglis, G., 1980. "What Will Oil Do to the Outports?" *The Rounder* Newfoundland and Labrador Rural Development Council, Vol. 6, No. 2, pp. 37-38.

Johnson, M.C., 1960. *The Effects of the Anaconda Aluminum Company Plant on Flathead County, Montana* Regional Study No. 12, Bureau of Business and Economic Research (Missoula MT: Montana State University).

Kaldor, D.R. and W.W. Bauder, 1963. "What Happpens when New Industry Comes to a Rural Community" *Iowa Farm Science*, Vol. 18, No. 5.

Kaldor, D.R., W.W. Bauder and M.W. Trautwein, 1964. *Impact of New Industry on an Iowa Rural Community, Part I: Farming and Farm Living* Spec. Rpt No. 37 (Iowa State University: Dept. of Econ. and Sociology).

Kerr, C. and A. Siegel, 1954. "The Inter-Industry Propensity to Strike" in D. Kornhauser et al. (eds.) Industrial Conflict (New York: Prentice-Hall).

Kirkenes, A. and O. Enkosen, 1976. Noen Regionale Konsekvenser av Rafinor (Bergen: Norwegian School of Economics and Admin.).

Kloppenburg, M., "Cooperative Housing: The Third Sector Option" Seminar paper, Faculty of Environmental Design, University of Calgary, 1982 (unpublished).

Kohrs, E.D.V., 1974. "Social Consequences of Boom Growth in Wyoming" Paper presented at the Rocky Mountain American Association of the Advancement of Science Meeting, Laramie, Wyoming, April 24-26.

Krahn, H. and J. Gartrell, 1981. "Labour Market Segmentation and Social Mobility in a Canadian Single-Industry Community" Canadian Review of Sociology and Anthropology

Krahn, H., J. Gartrell and L. Larson, 1981. "The Quality of Family Life in a Resource Community" Canadian Journal of Sociology, 6, pp. 307-324.

Kramer, R.M., 1969. Participation of the Poor (Englewood Cliffs, NJ: Prentice-Hall).

Kresge, D.T. and D.A. Siever, 1978. "Planning for a Resource-Rich Region: The Case of Alaska" The American Economic Review, Vol. 68, No. 2, pp. 99-103.

Kuznets, S., 1955. "Economic Growth and Income Inequality" American Economic Review, Vol. 45. pp. 1-28.

Lablebici, H. and G.r. Salancik, 1981. "Effects of environmental uncertainty on information and decision processes in banks" Administrative Science Quarterly, 26: 578-196.

Langerman, P.D., R.L. Byerly, and K.A. Root, 1982. Plant Closings and Layoffs: Problems Facing Urban and Rural Communities (Des Moines IA: College for Continuing Education, Drake University).

Lantz, H.R., 1958. People of Coal Town (New York: Columbia University Press).

Layton, M.R. and H.W. Ayer, 1972. "The Impacts of Mine Phase-Down and Redevelopment Policies on Local Communities: An Empirical Study" Paper presented at the Western Agricutural Economics Association Meetings, Logan, Utah, July 24.

Leistritz, F.L. and K.C. Maki, 1981. Socioeconomic Effects of Large-Scale Resource Development Projects in Rural Areas: The Case of McLean County, North Dakota (Fargo, ND: North Dakota State University).

Leistritz, F.L. and K.C. Maki, 1981. Socioeconomic Effects of Large-Scale Resource Development Projects in Rural Areas: The Case of

McLean County, North Dakota *Ag Econ Rpt. No. 151 (Fargo ND: North Dakota Agricultural Experiment Station).*

Leistritz, F.L. and R.A. Chase, 1981. "Socioeconomic Impact Monitoring Systems: Review and Recommendations" paper presented at Second International Forum on the Human Side of Energy, North Dakota State University, Fargo, ND.

Leistritz, F.L. and R.A. Chase, 1982. "Socioeconomic Impact Monitoring Systems: A Review and Evaluation" *Journal of Environmental Management* (in press).

Leistritz, F.L. and S.H. Murdock, 1981, *The Socioeconomic Impact of Resource Development: Methods for Assessment* (Boulder, CO: Westview Press).

Leistritz, F.L., D.D. Detomasi, J. Moore and S. Murdock, 1982a. "Induced Multiplier Effects" pp. 97-120 in Summers and Selvik (eds.) *Energy Resource Communities* (Madison WI: MJM Publishing Co.).

Leistritz, F.L., S.H. Murdock, N.E. Toman and D.M. Senechal, 1982b. "Local Fiscal Impacts of Energy Resource Development: Applications of an Assessment Model in Policy Making" *North Central Journal of Agricultural Economics,* Vol. 4, No. 1, pp. 47-57.

Levenson, R., *Company Towns: A Bibliography of American and Foreign Sources* (Monticello, Ill.: Council of Planning Librarians, 1977).

Lips, M., 1977. *Housing Cooperatives in Calgary* Faculty of Environmental Design, Master's Degree Project, University of Calgary (unpublished).

Little, R.L. and Stephen G. Lovejoy, 1979. "Energy Development and Local Employmnet" *The Social Science Journal,* Vol. 16(April): 27-37.

Little, R.L., 1977. "Some Social Consequencs of Boom Towns" *North Dakota Law Review,* 53, pp. 401-425.

Little, R.L., n.d. *Some Social Consequences of Boom Towns* (Logan UT: Utah State University).

Long, N.E., 1958. "The local community as an ecology of games" *American Journal of Sociology,* 44 (November): 251-266.

Long, N.E., 1962. *The Polity* (Chicago: Rand McNally).

Longbrake, G. and J.F. Geyler, 1979. "Commercial development in small isolated energy impacted communities" *Social Sciences Journal,* 16(2): 51-62.

Lucas, Rex, 1971. *Minetown, Milltown, Railtown: Life in Canadian Communities of Single Industry* (Toronto: U. of Toronto Press).

Luke, R.T., 1980. "Managing Community Acceptance of Major Industrial Projects" *Coastal Zone Management Journal,* 7: 271-296.

Luxton, M., 1980. *More than a Labour of Love* (Toronto: The Women's Press).

MWRI, 1982 is cited in Branch et al.,, but is not in their bibliography.

MacMillan, J.A., et al.,1974. *Determinants of Labour Turnover in Canadian Mining Communities (Winnipeg: Centre for Settlement Studies).*

Mackay, G.A., 1977. "The Local Economic and Employment Impacts of Landfall Terminals and Platform Construction in Scotland" in Occasional Paper 15/77 *Landfall Terminals and Local Communities* (Oslo: Norwegian Inst. of Urban and Regional Research).

Maguire, R.K., *Socioeconomic Factors Pertaining to Single-Industry Resource Towns in Canada: A Bibliography with Selected Annotations* Chicago: Council of Planning Librarians, 1980).

Maitland, S.T. and R.E. Friend, 1961. *Rural Industrialization* ERS, USDA, Bulletin No. 252.

Mansfield, E, 1963. "The speed of response of firms to new techniques" *Quarterly Journal of Economics*, 22 (May): 290-311.

Marans, R.W. and W. Rodgers, 1975. "Toward an Understanding of Community Satisfactions" pp. 299-352 in A.H. Hawley and V.P. Rock (eds.) *Metropolitan America in Contemporary Perspective* (New York: Wiley).

Marchak, P., 1979. "Labour in a Staples Economy" *Studies in Political Economy*, Vol. 2, pp. 7-36.

Martin, W.E., D. Deeds, E. Carpenter, H. Ayer, L. Arthur and R. Gum, 1976. *Reduction in Force in a Single Company Town: Who is Selected and How Do They Adapt?* Western Rural Development Center Discussion Paper No. 8, April (Corvallis, OR: Regional Center for Applied Social Science Research).

Matthiasson, J.S., 1970. *Resident Perceptions of Quality of Life in Resource Communities* , Series 2, No. 2 (Winnipeg: Centre for Settlement Studies).

Matthiasson, J.S., 1971. *Resident Mobility in resource Frontier Communities: An examination of Selected Factors* (Winnipeg, Man.: Winnipeg Centre for Settlement Studies, University of Manitoba).

Matthiasson, J.S., and Kerri, J.N., 1971. *Resident Mobility in Resource Frontier Communities: An Examination of Selected Factors* (Winnipeg: Centre for Settlement Studies, Report No. 6).

Mazza, J., 1982. *Shutdown: A Guide for Communities Facing Plant Closings* (Washington DC: Northeast-Midwest Institute).

McArthur, J.W. and R.O. Coppedge, 1969, "Employment Impacts of Industrial Development: A Case Study of Box Elder County, Utah from 1950 to 1966" *Utah Economic and Business Review*, Vol. 29, No. 2.

McCann, L.D., "The Changing Internal Structure of Canadian Resource Towns", *Plan Canada* 18(1978):46-59.

McCann, L.D., n.d. "Canadian Resource Towns: a Heartland-Hinterland Perspective", Department of Geography, Mountt Allison University, Sackville, New Brunswick. Unpublished mimeograph.

McKay, G.S., 1978. *The Economic Impact of North Sea Oil in Scotland* (London: Her Majesty's Stationery Office).

McKersie, R.B. and W.S. McKersie, 1982. *Plant Closings: What Can Be Learned from Best Practice* (Washington DC: Labor-Management Services Adminstration, U.S. Department of Labor).

McNicoll, I., 1982. "The Pattern of Oil Impact on Affected Scottish Rural Areas" Paper presented to the 17th Annual Conference of the Atlantic Association of Sociologists and Anthropologists.

McVey, W. and B.G. Ironside, 1978. *Migration within Alberta* (Edmonton, AB: Planning Secretariat, Advanced Education and Manpower, Government of Alberta).

Mellor, I. and R.G. Ironside, 1978. "The incidence Multiplier Impact of of Regional Development Programme" *Canadian Geographer*, XXII, 3.

Metz, W.C., 1979. *Socioeconomic Impact Management in the Western Energy Industry* BNL-25545 (Upton NY: Brookhaven National Laboratory).

Metz, W.C., 1980. "The Mitigation of Socioeconomic Impacts by Electric Utilities" *Public Utilities Fortnightly*, 106(1): 34-42.

Metz, W.C., 1981. *Construction Work Force Management: Worker Transportation and Temporary Housing Techniques* (Corvallis, OR: Western Rural Development Center).

Metz, W.C., 1982. "The Energy Industry's Involvement in Housing" in L. Kwit (ed.) *New Directions in Urban Energy Systems* (New York: Praeger Publishers, in press).

Miller, D.C., 1975. *Leadership and Power in Bos-Wash Megalopolis* (New York: Wiley).

Mills, C.W. and M.J. Ulmer, 1946. *Small Business and Civic Welfare* Report of the Small War Plants Corporation to the Special Committee to Study Problems of American Small Business. U.S. Senate, 79th Congress, 2nd Session, Document Number 135. Serial No. 11036 (Washington, DC: U.S. Government Printing Office).

Moe, I., 1972. *Storbedrifter: Lokalsamfunn, Storbedrifter Innvirkning pa Pendling, Flytting og Naeringstrukter: Stord og Kvinnherad* (Bergen: Dept. of Geography).

Mohr, L.B., 1969. "Determinants of innovation in organization" *American Political Science Review*, 63 (March): 111-126.

Molnar, 1978 is cited in Branch, but is not in bibliography.

Moore, K.D., 1979. *Simulating Energy-Related Growth: Models, Uncertainty, and the Local Response* (Denver CO: Denver Research Institute).

Moore, R. (ed.), 1981. *Labour Migration and Oil* Occasional paper No. 7 (London: Social Science Research Council, North Sea Panel).

Moriarty, B.M., 1980. *Industrial Location and Community Development* (Chapel Hill NC: University of North Carolina Press).

Morrell, D. and C. Magorian, 1982. *Siting Hazardous Waste Facilities: Local Opposition and the Myth of Pre-emption* (Princeton, NJ: Center for Energy and Environmental Studies, Princeton University).

Mountain West Research, Inc., 1975. *Construction Worker Profile* (Washington, DC: Old West Regional Commission).

Mountain West Research, Inc., 1979a. *A Guide to Methods for Impact Assessment of Western Coal/Energy Development* January.

Mountain West Research, Inc., 1979b. *Mineral Fuels Taxation in the Old West Reiong* Prepared for the University of Montana under a grant from the Old West Regional Commission, Billings, MT.

Mountain West Research, Inc., 1980. *BLM Social Effects Project Abridged Literature Review"* Prepared for the Bureau of Land Management, pp. 148-150.

Mountain West Research, Inc., 1981. "Socioeconomic Impacts of Western Coal Development" (Draft) Prepared for the Bureau of Land Management, Billings, MT.

Murdock, S.H. and E.C. Schriner, 1978. "Structural and Distributional Factors in Community Development" *Rural Sociology*, 43(3), pp. 426-449.

Murdock, S.H. and F.L. Leistritz, 1979. *Energy Development in the Western United States: Impact on Rural Areas* (New York: Praeger Publishers).

Murray, J.A., 1980. "The effects of rapid population growth on the provision and financing of local public services" Paper presented to the seminar on Coping with Rapid Growth, Scottsdale, Arizona.

Myhra, D., 1980. *Energy Plant Sites: Community Planning for Large Projects* (Atlanta GA: Conway Publications, Inc.).

Myklebost, H., 1969. *Fellebygdene som Arbeidsplass of Arbeidskraftreserve* Ad Notat Nr. 8 (Oslo: Universitats Forlaget).

NORDCO, 1982. *Study of the Political Socio-Economic Effects on the Newfoundland Fishing Industry From Offshore Petroleum Development* (St. John's, Nfld.: Newfoundland Oceans Research and Development Corporation).

Nellis, L., 1974. "What Does Energy Development Mean for Wyoming?"

Human Organization, Vol. 30, No. 3, pp. 229-238.

Nelson, G., 1979. "Distributional Issues in Community Growth Impact Models" pp. 17-42 in Hushak and Morse (eds.) *Proceedings of the Ex Ante Growth Impact Models Conference* (Ames IA: Iowa State University).

Newby, H., 1977. *The Deferential Worker* (London: Allen Lane).

Newby, H., 1982. "A Sociological Approach" pp. 1-22 in Summers and Selvik (eds.) *Energy Resource Communities* (Madison WI: MJM Publishing Co.).

Newfoundland and Labrador Federation of Labour, 1978. *Now That We've Burned Our Boats...The Report of the Peoples's Commission on Unemployment* (St. John's, Nfld.).

Newfoundland and Labrador, Government of, 1977. "An Act Respecting Petroleum and Natural Gas".

Newfoundland and Labrador, Government of, 1978. "Newfoundland and Labrador Petroleum Regulation, 1977" *Newfoundland Gazette*, November 10, 1978. (St. John's, Nfld.)

Newfoundland and Labrador, Government of, 1980. "Petroleum Resource Potential of Offshore Newfoundland and Labrador" Petroleum Directorate Special Report 80-2.

Newfoundland and Labrador, Government of, 1981a. "Newfoundland and Labrador Petroleum Regulations 1977" (Amendment). *Newfoundland Gazette*, November 6, 1981.

Newfoundland and Labrador, Government of, 1981b. "The Petroleum Potential of the western Newfoundland Onshore Area" Petroleum Directorate Special Report 81-2.

Newfoundland and Labrador, Government of, 1981c. "Economic Impact of Future Offshore Petroleum Exploration" Joint Report of the Department of Development and the Petroleum Directorate.

Newfoundland and Labrador, Government of, 1981d. "An Introduction to Oil-Related Onshore Developments" Provincial Planning Office, Department of Development.

Nichols, P.C. and Associates, Ltds., 1981. *A Study of Social Impact in the Lower Peace, North Peace, and East Peace Sub-Regions* (Edmonton: Northern Alberta Development Council).

Northern B.C. Women's Task Force, 1978. *Northern B.C. Women's Task Force report on Single Industry Resource Communities* Vancouver, B.C.: Women's Research Centre, Mimeo.

O'Hare, M., D. Sanderson and L.S. Bacow, 1982. *Facility Siting* (New York: Van Nostraind-Reinhold, in press).

Olson, D.A. and J.A. Kuehn, 1974. *Migrant Response to Industrialization in Four Rural Areas, 1965-70* Agricultural Economics Report No. 270

(Washington DC: USDA, Economic Research Service in cooperation with the University of Missouri).

Outcrop Ltd., 1981. *Dome/Canmar Beaufort Sea Operations: An Economic Analysis 1976-1980* Unpublished report (Yellowknife NWT:
Outcrop Ltd.)

PRAXIS (A Social Planning Company) *Resource Community Study* Proposal for Canstar Oil Sands Company Ltd., in association with Dr.
George Kupper and Dr. Ira Robinson, Calgary, Alberta, August
1982.

Paden, D., D. Krist and M. Seaton, 1972. *Impact of Industrial Development on Selected Iowa Communities* (Ames IA: Iowa Development
Commission).

Pahl, R.E., 1971. *Whose City?* (London: Longmans).

Parker, V. J., 1960. *The Planned Non Permanent Community: An Approach to Development of New Towns Based on Mining Activity*
Ottawa: Northern Coordination and Research centre, Department
of Indian Affairs and Natural Resources, June, 1963. Also, unpublished Master's Thesis, University of British Columbia, Vancouver,
1960.

Parkinson, A. and Detomasi, D.D., "Planning Resource Towns for the
Alberta Tar Sands" *Plan Canada* 20 (1980).

Parkinson, Anna and D.D. Detomasi, "Planning Resource Towns for the
Alberta Tar Sands" *Plan Canada* , Vol. 20, No. 2, June 1980, pp.
91-102.

Parson, T., 1951. *The Social System* (New York: The Free Press).

Peelle, E., 1979. "Mitigating Community Impacts of Energy Development:
Some Examples for Coal and Nuclear Generating Plants in the
United States" Paper presented at the 1979 Annual Meeting of the
American Association for the Advancement of Science, Houston,
Texas, January 3.

Pickvance, C.G. (ed.), 1976. *Urban Sociology: Critical Essays* (London:
Tavistock).

Porteous, D., *Residents' Attitudes Towards and Perceptions of the Quality of Life in British Columbia Resource Towns* (Victoria, U. of
Victoria, Department of Geography, 1974).

Porteous, J.D., "Quality of Life in British COlumbia Company Towns" in
New Communities in Canada: Exploring Planned Environments N.
Pressman, ed. *Contact* 8, No. 3 (Special Issue, 1976) 170-88.

Pressman, N.E. "A Selected Bibliography on New Towns" *Plan Canada* 2
(1972), 161-66.

Pressman, N.E., 1976. "Social Planning Prerequisites in New and Expanded Communities" in N. Pressman (ed.) *New Communities in
Canada: Exploring Planned Environments* Special Issue, *Contact*,
8, 170-88.   ·

Pressman, Norman E.P., "Social Perspectives on Planned Development: North American Experience" *Contact* Special Issue–International Settlement Strategies: Social Perspectives on Planned Development, Vol. 10, No. 3, Winter 1978, pp. 1-85.

Pritchard, N., 1967. "Planned Social Provision in New Towns" *Town Planning Review*, 38, 26-34.

Rabnett, R.A. and Associates, 1978. *Resource Community Planning: A Framework for Choosing Settlement Options* (Victoria: British Columbia Department of Municipal Affairs).

Rabnett, R.A. and Skaburskis, A., 1977. *Alternative Methods of Financing and Developing Resource Based Communities* for Thompson, Berwick, Pratt and Partners (Victoria: B.C. Department of Municipal Affairs).

Rein, M., 1980. "Fact and function in human service organizations" *Sociology and Social Research*, 65: 78-93.

Reinschmiedt and Jones, 1973 is cited once in Pulver, but is not in the bibliography. This may be a typo in the text.

Reinschmiedt, L. and L.L. Jones, 1977. "Impact of Industrialization on Employee Income Distribution in Rural Texas Communities" *Southern Journal of Agricultural Economics*, Vol. 9, No. 2, pp. 67-72.

Ricchiardi, S., 1982. "The Children of the Unemployed" *Des Moines Sunday Register*, May 9, p. 1.

Rice, D., D. Saxowsky and F.L. Leistritz, 1980. *Probable Effects of Nuclear Repository Study Site Designation on Local Land Values and Precedents/Procedures for Indemnification of Affected Parties* (Fargo ND: North Dakota State University, Department of Agricultural Economics).

Riffel, J.A., *Quality of Life in Resource Towns, (Ottawa: Ministry of State for Urban Affairs, 1975)*.

Rink, R. and Ford, A., *A Simulation Model for Boomtown Housing* LA-7324-MS (Los Alamos: Los Alamos Scientific Lab., 1978).

Roberts, L.W., 1977. "Wage Employment in Two Easter Arctic Communities. Ph.D. Thesis Submitted to the Faculty of Graduate Studies and Research Department of Sociology, University of Alberta, Edmonton, AB.

Robinson, A., 1976 is referred to in Detomasi, but is not in Bibliography.

Robinson, I., et al., "A Trade-Off Approach for Eliciting Environmental References" in D. Carson ed., *Man Environmenta Environment Interactions: Evaluations and Applicatins* (Stroudsburg, Pa.: Dowden Hutchinson and Ross, 1975).

Robinson, I.M., 1962. *New Industrial Towns on Canada's Resource Frontier* Research Paper No. 73 (Chicago IL: The Univeristy of Chicago, Department of Geography).

Robinson, I.M., 1973. "Small Independent, Self-Contained and Balanced New Towns: Myth or Reality?" Chapter I in Perloff and Sandberg (eds.) *New Towns–Why and For Whom*, (Proeger).

Robinson, I.M., 1979. "Planning, Building, Managing New Towns on the Resource Frontier" in W.T. Perks and Ira Miles Robinson (eds.) *Urban and Regional Planning in a Federal State: The Canadian Experience* (Stroudsburg, PA: Dowden, Hutchinson & Ross Inc.).

Rogers, D.L. and B.F. Pendleton, 1979. "The role of community services in community theory: A critique of literature on community services and a suggested paradigm" Paper presented to the Rural Sociolog-cial Society, Burlington, Vermont.

Rogers, D.L., B.F. Pendleton, W.J. Goudy and R.O. Richards, 1978. "Industrialization, Income Benefits and the Rural Community" *Rural Sociology*, 43(2), pp. 250-264.

Rokkan, S., 1966. "Numerical democracy and corporate pluralism" in R.A. Dahl (ed.) *Political Oppositions in Western Democracies* (New Haven: Yale University Press).

Root, K.S., 1978. "job Loss and Job Losers: Variability in Response to Displacement" Paper presented at the Annual Meetin of the Society for the Study of Social Problems: Labor Studies Division, San Francisco, CA, September 1-4.

Root, K.S., 1979. *Companies, Mines, and Factories–Shutdowns, Closures, and Moves: A Bibliography* (Monticello IL: Vance Bibliographies).

Rossi, P., R. Berk and B. Edison, 1974. *The Roots of Urban Discontent* (New York: Wiley).

Sahota, G.S., 1978. "Theories of Personal Income Distribution: A Survey" *Journal of Economic Literature*, Vol. XVI, pp. 1-55.

Sanderson, D.R., 1979. *Compensation in Facility Siting Conflicts* MIT Energy Impacts Project Document #11 (Cambridge MA: Massachusetts Institute of Technology).

Scott, J.T. Jr. and G.F. Summers, 1974. "Problems in Rural Communities after Industry Arrives" *Rural Industrialization: Problems and Potentials* (Ames IA: Iowa State University Press).

Seiver, D.A., 1981. "Projecting the Income Distribution in a Regional Economy" *Growth and Change*, pp. 9-15.

Selvik, A., 1982. "Energy Resource Communities: Inflationary Tendencies" pp. 189-198 in Summers and Selvik (eds.) *Energy Resource Communities* Madison WI: MJM Publishing Co.).

Selvik, A. and G. Hernes, 1977. *Dynamikk: Borehullene Om Kraftutbygging og Lokal Samfum* (Bergen: Universitats Forlaget).

Shaffer, R.E. and D.W. Fischer, 1981. *Evaluating Local-National Impacts from Landing Statfjkord Gas* (Bergen, Norway: The Institute of Industrial Economics).

Shaffer, R.E., 1974. "Rural Industrialization: A Local Income Analysis" *Southern Journal of Agricultural Economics*, pp. 97-102.

Shaffer, R.E., D. Fisher and G.C. Pulver, 1982. "Capturing Secondary Benefits of Economic Development" pp. 121-140 in G. Summers and A. Selvik (eds.) *Energy Resource Communities* (Madison WI: MJM Publishing).

Siemens, L.B., 1976. "Single Enterprise Communities on Canada's Resource Frontier" in N. Pressman (ed.) *New Communities in Canada: Exploring Planned Environments* Special Issue *Contact*, 8, No.3.

Sommers, G., 1958. "Labor Recruitment in a Depressed Rural Area" *Monthly Labor Reivew*, Vol. 81, No. 10, 1113-1120.

State of California, 1982. *Planning Guidebook for Communities Facing a Plant Closure or Mass Layoff* (Sacramento CA: Employment Development Department, Office of Planning and Policy Development).

Stelter, G. and Artibise, A., 1978. "Canadian Resource Towns in Historical Perspective" *Plan Canada* 18, 7-16.

Stenstavold, K., 1979. "Recruitment to Oil Related Activities in Norway: A Preliminary Analysis of Recruitment Distances" in J. Sewell (ed.) *The Promis and the Reality of Large Scale Developments in Marginal Regions* (Aberdeen Scotland: Inst. for the Study of Sparsely Populated Areas).

Stevens, J.B. and L.T. Wallace, 1964. *Impact of Industrial Development on Howard County, Indiana* Research BUlletin No. 784 (Lafayette, IN: Purdue University).

Stevenson, D.S., 1968. *Problems of Eskimo Relocation for Industrial Employment* (Ottawa: Northern Science Research Group, Department of Indian Affairs and Northern Development).

Strange, W., 1978. "Job Loss: A Psychosocial Study of Worker Reactions to a Plant-Closing in a Company Town in Southern Appalachia" Ph.D. Dissertation, Cornell University.

Summers, G. and K. Branch, 1982. "Human Responses to Energy Development" pp. 23-59 in G.F. Summers and A. Selvik (eds.) *Energy Resource Communities* (Bergen, Norway: MJM Publishing Co.).

Summers, G.F. and A. Selvik, 1979. *Nonmetropolitan Industrial Growth and Community Change* (Cambridge MA: Lexington Books).

Summers, G.F. and A. Selvik, 1982. *Energy Resource Communities* (Madison WI: MJM Publishing Co. for The Institute of Industrial Economics, Bergen, Norway).

Summers, G.F. and F. Clemente, 1976. "Industrial Development, Income Distribution and Public Policy" Rural Sociology, 41(2) pp. 248-268.

Summers, G.F., 1973. "Large Industry in a Rural Area: Demographic, Economic, and Social Impacts" Working Paper RID 7.3.19 (Madison WI: Center for Applied Sociology, University of Wisconsin-Madison).

Summers, G.F., S. Evans, J. Minkoss, F. Clemente and E.M. Beck, 1976. Industrial Invasion of Nonmetropolitan America: A Quarter Century of Experience (New York: Praeger Pub.).

Summers, G.F., S.D. Evans, F. Clemente, E.M. Beck and J. Minkoff, 1976. Industrial Invasion of Nonmetropolitan America: A Quarter Century of Experience (New York: Praeger Publishers).

Swerdloff, S., 1980. A Guide for Communities Facing Major Layoffs or Plant Shutdowns (Washington DC: U.S. Deparmtent of Labor, Employment and Training Administration).

Syvertsen, P. and M. Tuder, 1976. Kraftutbygging og Lokale Vare of Tjenesteleveranser Occasional Paper 5/76 (Oslo: Norwegian Inst. of Urban and Regional Research).

Teague, C.H., 1980. "Plant Closure: A Case History Testimony before the U.S. Senate Committee on Labor and Human Resources, Washington, DC, September 17.

Thompson, J.G., A.L. Blevins and G.L. Watts, 1978. "Socioeconomic Longitudinal Monitoring Report (Washington DC: Old West Regional Commission).

Thompson, J.R., 1980. "Economic Organization in Abridged Literature Review: BLM Social Effects Project (Billings MT: Mountain West Research Inc.).

Tilly, C., 1973. "Do communities act? Sociological Inquiry, 43 (December): 209-237.

Turner, R.J. and Gartrell, J.W., 1978. "Social Factors in Psychiatric Outcomes: Towards the Resolution of Interpretive Controversieš American Sociological Review, 43, pp. 368-382.

Urban Systems Research and Engineering, Inc., 1980. A Handbook for the States on the Use of Compensation and Incentives in the Siting of Hazardous Waste Management Facilities (Cambridge MA: Urban Systems Research and Engineering Inc.).

Van Dyke, E.W. and Loberg, C., 1978 Community Studies: Fort McMurray, Anzac, Fort McKay (Edmonton: Alberta Oil Sands Environmental Research Program, Alberta Environment).

Vatne, E., 1979. Solospill Eller Samspill? En Underso /kelse av Industrenbedrifter Samhandling sam Strategi for Regional Utvikling Working Rept. Nr. 19 (Bergen: Inst. Industrial Economics).

Vatne, E., 1980. "Structural Change, Industrial Linkages and Production Systems: The Case of a One-Company Town Paper presented at the meeting of the IGU Commission on Industrial Systems, Tokyo, Japan, August 25-31.

Vatne, E., 1981. "Single Sector Economies: The Resources Base Trap̃ Paper presented at the Sixth International Seminar on Marginal Regiona, Bergen/Sogndal, Norway, August 6-12.

Vatne, E., 1982. "Local Production Networkš pp. 155-168 in Summers and Selvik (eds.) Energy Resource Communities (Madison WI: MJM Publishing Co.).

Veit, Suzanne nd Associates Labour Turnover and Community Stability Report to the Federal-Provincial Manpower Subcommittee on Northeast Coal Development, 1977/78. Proj. No. 2700060-3. February 1978.

Vidich and Bensman is cited in Branch et al., but is not in their bibliography.

Walton, J., 1967. "The vertical axis of community organization and the structure of poweř Social Science Quarterly, 48 (December): 353-368.

Warner, W.K., 1979. "Rural society in a postindustrial agě Rural Sociology, 39: 306-318.

Warren, D.I., 1975. Black Neighborhoods: An Assessment of Community Power (Ann Arbor: University of Michigan Press).

Warren, R.L., 1966. Perspectives on the American Community (New York: Rand McNally).

Warren, R.L., 1978. The Community in America Third Edition (Chicago: Rand-McNally).

Weber, B.A. and R. Howell, 1982. Coping with Rapid Growth (Boulder CO: Westview Press).

Werner, B., 1980. A Survey of the Socia and Economic Effects of Oil and Gas Development: Little Missouri National Grasslands, North Dakota RI-80-28, U.S. Forest Service.

Wichern, P.H. et al. 1971. The Production and Testing of a Model of Political Development in Resource Frontier Communities Research Report NO. 4 (Winnipeg: University of Manitoba, Centre for Settlement Studies).

Wieland, J.S., F.L. Leistritz and S.H. Murdock, 1979. "Characteristics and Residential Patterns of Energy-Related Work Forces in the Northern Great Plainš Western Journal of Agricultural Economics, 4(1): 57-68.

Wilber, G.L. and S.T. Maitland, 1963. Industrialization in Chickasaw County, Mississippi: A Study of Rural Residents (State College, MS: Mississippi State University).

Wilkenson, P., J.G. Thompson, R.R. Reynolds Jr. and L.M. Ostrech, 1982. "Local Social Disruption and Western Energy Developmenť Pacific Sociological Review, 25, pp. 275-296.

Wilkinson, K. and J. Thompson, 1981. *Craig, Colorado: BLM Social Effects Project* (Laramie, WY: Wyoming Research Corporation).

Williams, R., 1973. *The Country and the City* (London: Chatto and Windus).

Williamson, Robert G., 1974. *Eskimo Underground: Socio-Cultural Change in the Canadian Central Arctic* (Uppsala: Institutionen For Allman Och Jamforande Etnografi Vid Uppsala Universitet).

Wirt, F.M., 1974. *Power in the City* (Berkeley: University of California Press).

Index

190